Finding Our Way

Finding Our Way

Creating Change in Ourselves and Our Relationships

DR. LARRY COHEN
Therapist & Life Coach

The SBC Press

Published and distributed by The SBC Press, info@thesbcpress.com

Bookstores contact:
The SBC Press, orders@thesbcpress.com

Personal orders available:
Amazon.com or
email your request to orders@thesbcpress.com

ISBN 13: 9798391796312

For more information, contact:
The SBC Press
532 Marlton Pike W.
Suite 106
Marlton, NJ 08053

Or

Dr. Larry Cohen
4 N. Maple Ave.
Marlton, NJ 08053
(856) 352-5428
info@drlarrycohen.com
www.drlarrycohen.com

CONTENTS

PART TWO: OUR RELATIONSHIPS

DEDICATION

For my wife, Renee. Thank you for accepting me for who I am.

For my parents, who have stood with me always.

For my clients, who inspire me each day and allow me to witness the miraculous changes people can make.

In memory of my best friend, Michael.

Introduction

"It takes courage to grow up and turn out to be who you really are."

— E.E. Cummings

I have had the privilege of being a psychotherapist and life coach for 30 years. During that time, I have worked with individuals and couples, helping them overcome problems that prevent them from living happy and healthy lives. Working on ourselves is essential to finding our way, and working on our relationships is another.

This book has two parts. The first, "Ourselves," focuses on what I teach people to help them change themselves. In these chapters, I write about how to build self-worth, combat negative thinking, stop perfectionism, worry less, and set protective and family boundaries. In the second part, "Our Relationships," I look at how to rediscover intimacy, learn to be best friends again, pick your partner, have a successful long-term relationship, how to establish trust, and more.

I provide a worksheet at the end of each chapter so that you can quickly reflect on what you've read, write down the changes you'd like to make in your life and list the steps you need to take to make those changes. The chapters in each section are individual essays and can be read in any order.

As a therapist, I have worked with people with childhood trauma, depression, anxiety, relationship problems, and other issues. Psychotherapy, rooted in psychological theories and clinical practice, focuses on resolving or reducing emotional pain and mental health problems. I use two methods in therapy: psychodynamic psychotherapy and cognitive therapy.

In psychodynamic psychotherapy, I help people resolve the emotions associated with past traumas. I work on changing how you see the past and your perspective on it. This work enables you to process emotions related to past traumas and lessen or resolve their impact on your life today. We question clouded, distorted views you may have about yourself and your relationships due to developmental trauma.

In cognitive therapy, I help clients identify their beliefs about themselves, how these beliefs cloud their thinking, and how this clouded view of reality drives emotions and behaviors. Having an understanding of how you see yourself and how you think allows you to challenge your faulty thinking and correct it. As a result, emotions and behaviors change. In addition, correcting faulty thinking enables you to choose your behaviors. Instead of reacting, you can begin to choose how to behave. As a result, you act instead of react. This work can change your life as it adds greater choice to how you live.

I always provide therapy using what is called a person-centered approach. Person-centered therapy, pioneered by Carl Rogers, emphasizes the power of empathy, genuineness, and unconditional positive regard in facilitating personal growth. This approach centers on creating a non-judgmental, empathic therapeutic alliance, allowing you to explore your past experiences, uncover your inherent strengths, and find solutions. It promotes self-acceptance, self-empowerment, and the cultivation of authentic self-expression.

As a life coach, I help people identify life goals, uncover the steps to achieving them, and work to overcome the obstacles that prevent them from reaching their goals. Life coaching embraces a forward-looking perspective, focusing on personal development, goal setting, and achieving desired outcomes. It aims to enhance individual strengths, clarify values, and inspire you to take purposeful action toward your aspirations. Life coaching empowers you to live authentically, cultivate resilience, and design a fulfilling life aligned with your values and goals.

In "Finding Our Way," I share what I teach clients daily. This book will challenge your thinking and how you see yourself and your relationships. I hope it helps you uncover your true self, change your ways of seeing, and live the life you imagine.

May 18, 2023

PART ONE: OURSELVES

"You are braver than you believe, stronger than you seem and smarter than you think!"

— Christopher Robin

1. SELF-WORTH

Freedom From Codependence

To live a happy, joyful life, it is essential to establish lasting, positive feelings of self-worth. Some of us have steady feelings of worth and value, while others experience fluctuating feelings of self-worth and struggle to control the highs and lows.

A fluctuating, unstable sense of self is experienced when your self-worth depends on things outside of yourself, like your job, how much money you have, or your lifestyle. If this is you, then you are what is called codependent. A codependent relies on things outside of themselves to provide feelings of self-worth.

No matter how much you believe they are, things like your job or how much money you have are not within your control. Relying on them to provide self-worth can eventually make your life feel out of control as you try to control uncontrollable things. Codependence affects your self-worth because negative things lower it while positive things increase it. To fight off the ups and downs of codependence, you must maintain an inner sense of self-worth. When you do, you are free from codependence, and what is happening outside of you does not define you.

Codependence Broadly Defined

When I think of codependence, I immediately think about addiction and how addiction impacts the family. Addiction theory defines codependence as what the addict's partner experiences simply by being the partner of an addict. This type of codependence manifests when the addict's partner allows their emotions and daily life to revolve around that of the addict. If the addict is doing well, they are doing well. If the addict is doing poorly, they suffer. But this is only one kind of codependence. Here, I am looking at a broader definition of codependence.

Dependence on things outside of yourself can cause you to feel that your life is out of your control. Your inner world and your sense of self-worth fluctuate as your outer world changes.

My definition of codependence includes dependence on things outside of yourself that impact your sense of self-worth and sometimes even define it. You can be codependent on your job, money, or the people you surround yourself with.

For example, losing a job can be devastating, but your entire sense of self-worth can collapse if you are codependent on your job. As important as a job is, it does not define who you are. You may also be a partner or parent; we are all sons or daughters. I have worked with codependents who were highly sought-after professionals. Even though they could find other work, they could not accept what had happened. One, a mother of four, was so devastated by her job loss that she couldn't value how much her children loved her. She was so codependent on her career that she could only think about the job she lost ten months earlier. She told me she felt like a complete failure.

Even this - loving others and being loved - is not who you are. You are not what you do or what you give. You are valuable just for being born. Your self-worth is something inside, not something defined by things on the outside.

Being dependent on things outside of yourself leads, at best, to a fluctuating sense of self-worth. You forfeit your ability to find the self-worth that comes from within. Your codependence must be stopped to have consistent, positive feelings of self-worth.

Negative Core Beliefs

Your core beliefs are those things you believe about yourself deep down. These beliefs drive and play a significant role in codependence. Negative core beliefs include "I am a failure" or "I am not as good as other people." For example, someone who is a 'caretaker' may have the core belief "I am unlovable," or "My happiness depends on making others happy," or "I am only valuable if I am needed by someone else." The caretaker is codependent on being able to take care of someone else to feel loved. These beliefs drive a caretaker to prioritize others' needs above their own and seek validation and self-worth by caring for others.

Codependence and Fluctuating Self-Worth

When you are codependent, your self-worth can fluctuate from high to low very quickly when life experiences don't turn out how you expect them to. For example, you go out on a date with someone you believe is perfect for you - you dream of a beautiful life together and feel fantastic. Eventually, however, you discover this person isn't who you thought they were and decide this is not 'your person.' As a result, you start thinking that you'll never meet someone, blame yourself, and think there must be something wrong with YOU. This triggers the inner core belief that you are a loser. Your sense of self-worth drops as a result. Another example: you expect a promotion at work, and your boss passes you over and gives the job to someone else. Because you are codependent, you think you're not good enough and will never get a promotion.

Both examples are difficult, and if you define who you are and how valuable you are by uncontrollable life circumstances such as these, you are codependent. Inner core beliefs such as "I am a failure," "I am worthless," or "my life will never get better" strongly re-enforce feelings of low self-worth. In these examples, codependence on your relationships and job becomes self-defining, and feelings of positive self-worth diminish.

Codependence as Teeter-Tauter

Codependence on positive things can also affect your self-worth. For example, you do receive the desired promotion and a substantial pay raise. You feel like a success and great about yourself and your future. Your feelings of positive self-worth feel solid, and your self-esteem and confidence increase. However, yesterday you considered finding a new job because you weren't enjoying your work. As time passes, you enjoy the promotion and its benefits, but soon you feel you still dislike your job and want to find another one.

Even though your life improves in certain ways due to your promotion, your sense of self-worth decreases over time. Things worsen as some of your negative core beliefs arise. You ask yourself, "Why am I still stuck in this job? There must be something better out there." You begin a job search. Six months later, you are still dissatisfied and unable to find a better job. Feelings of failure increase, and your sense of self-worth continues to drop.

Your promotion, which initially bolstered positive feelings of self-worth, no longer provides positive validation. Your sense of self-worth, which you believed to be high, dropped over time as you realized that the raise and other benefits of the promotion didn't lead to happiness. Being codependent and relying on your job to bolster your self-worth didn't work. Disappointments are inevitable if you depend on things outside yourself to provide positive worth. These are things that you cannot control.

Whether positive or negative, dependence on things outside yourself creates ups and downs and makes you feel that your life is out of your control. Your inner world and sense of self-worth fluctuate as your outer world changes. This is the powerful influence of codependence.

An Inside Job - How to Make Cognitive and Behavioral Changes

'It's an inside job' is something we've all heard. But, it is true. Positive feelings of self-worth must come from within. Codependence on things outside of yourself - that you have relied on to feel good about yourself - must go. Changing this requires a change in perspective. You must learn to value things outside of yourself less. But, this can feel unfamiliar and even wrong. It is necessary, however, if you are to find happiness and positive self-worth.

The road to increasing and stabilizing your sense of self-worth begins by digging deep and identifying your negative core beliefs. I tell people they must vigorously challenge their negative core beliefs to build positive self-worth. If, at your core, you believe that you are 'worthless,' take steps to challenge that belief fully. Is this belief something you were born with? Unlikely. Did someone else teach you to believe this about yourself? Probably. Are you really worthless? If the answer is no, learn to challenge your negative core beliefs when they come up. Ask yourself, "Is there evidence to support my belief about myself?" If it's true, work on personal change. But, if there is no evidence to support your negative core belief, work to discover why you believe it and shed it.

You are not born with negative core beliefs about yourself. These beliefs are often taught, forced upon you, or formed by negative life experiences.

Take time to identify and challenge your negative core beliefs and explore the origins of those beliefs. You are not born with negative core beliefs about yourself. These beliefs are often taught, forced upon us, or formed by negative life experiences. Be kind to yourself and work hard to identify and change your negative core belief systems. Doing this work is essential if you are to find greater happiness.

Uncovering and Quantifying Your Value as a Person

Loving people care for, celebrate, and affirm others. Hateful people hurt others by deflecting their self-hatred onto others. Do not believe the negative things others taught you or have you believe about yourself. The judgment of others is not yours. Be careful not to take it inside. Why should you? It did not come from within you. I tell people, "Just because it was handed to you doesn't mean you have to carry it with you."

I always instruct my clients to fight off and correct their negative core beliefs by using affirmations. Examples include: 'I am valuable,' 'I am enough just as I am,' and 'I am a good, loving person.' Remember: mean, emotionally abusive people weren't born that way. They became that way.

Self-Worth Defined. Internalizing Your Value as a Person

The past is gone, the present is a gift, and the future is limitless. Take control of your life by letting go of codependence. Uncover and re-integrate the inherent worth and value you were born with. Embrace your worth and do the work necessary to re-discover and rebuild a positive sense of self-worth. Being valuable and worthwhile is your birthright. Once found, diligently guard your newfound sense of self-worth, and don't let anyone make you forget about what has always been yours.

Reflections

What changes do you want to make?

_____

_____

_____

_____

_____

_____

_____

What steps do you need to take to bring about change?

_____

_____

_____

_____

_____

_____

_____

_____

_____

"The willingness to accept responsibility for one's own life is the source from which self-respect springs."

— Joan Didion

2. TAKING RESPONSIBILITY

Create Lasting Life Changes

My therapy and life coaching clients who grow and achieve the most, and are most satisfied with their therapeutic and life coaching experience, understand the need to accept personal responsibility. You must take responsibility for your life choices to create lasting life changes. You must also accept who you were, who you are, and who you want to be.

Once you accept and understand that you and you alone are responsible for your life, you have the freedom to make tremendous life changes. Taking full responsibility for who you are allows you to grow, change, and be who you want to be. Your choices are no longer limited. You can be who you choose.

Taking responsibility for yourself can be a challenge. It requires you to accept all of your life and yourself, the good and the bad. Once you fully understand and accept that you are solely responsible for your life, great responsibility follows. You are responsible for yourself and in charge of making the changes necessary to improve your life.

Take Control

When you begin accepting personal responsibility, you see that blaming others for your problems seems foolish and a waste of energy. Now that you fully control your own life, it is up to you to create life changes. This was always possible, but it may have eluded you - that only you can create change in your life. When you understand and accept responsibility for yourself and your life, past fantasies of being saved and fixed by others vanish.

You may have been convinced that others knew what was best for you and that others were responsible for taking care of you. However, accepting full responsibility for your life means fixing and improving yourself. Working with a life coach will help you find the guidance you need to discover and get where you want to be.

If you believe your problems are someone else's fault, you may expect others to see how they've wronged you and then remorsefully save you from your despair. The problem with blaming life's difficulties on others is that you hand over the responsibility for your happiness to them. You can only sit and wait for them to change. Since they did you wrong, only they have the power to make it right. When you accept personal responsibility for your happiness, you break away from your reliance on others and gain the ability to create change and improve your life. Although being responsible for your own happiness may feel foreign, in time, you will wonder why you didn't take responsibility for your life sooner.

Shed Victimhood

Victims stew, waiting for their life to improve. They continue to hope and wait for the person whose behavior leads to their unhappiness to make things right. Victims believe their life can only improve if the person they believe is responsible for their unhappy life changes.

When you begin accepting personal responsibility, you see that blaming others for your problems seems foolish and a waste of energy.

One example might be, "If I weren't stuck in this lousy job, I would be much happier. My boss is disrespectful and doesn't value what I offer." Here, the victim hands responsibility for happiness to the boss, waiting for the boss to deliver a happier, more satisfying life. Is it realistic to believe that the boss will change his behavior, provide a more enjoyable work environment, and begin respecting you? Or, is it in your best interest to accept personal responsibility for your job dissatisfaction, make appropriate life changes, and find a new job?

Own Your Life

Taking personal responsibility for past failures, past mistreatment of others, and past irresponsible behavior is essential. The feelings of shame and guilt you may feel need to be put to good use. Use these feelings to guide your behaviors. Healthy shame and guilt uncover behaviors you will not repeat.

But, of course, it's much easier to blame others and live the life of a victim. You can blame everyone else for your unhappiness if you are a victim. But thinking like a victim strips you of your ability to solve your problems and change your life.

15

Blaming others puts your life in someone else's hands and forces you to give away your personal power and self-respect. It's time to change your old ways, break away, and figure things out for yourself. Grab hold, accept personal responsibility, and never again put your dream of a better life in someone else's hands.

Blaming others puts your life in someone else's hands and forces you to give away your personal power and self-respect.

Find a Better Tomorrow

Moving forward, you must set your own life goals, identify the steps to achieve them, and follow through by taking action. This is your responsibility, as you hold the key to your happiness and success. A life coach can help you identify your goals, the life changes you want, and how to reach them.

Are you ready to move forward? Take time to answer the following questions. They may motivate you to act and move you forward toward needed change.

- Are you a victim, or are you a survivor?

- Are you ready to begin the transformation process?

- Do you accept personal responsibility for your life?

- Have you let go of the fantasy that someone else will fix your life?

Many of us may have blamed someone or something else for the problems we face in our lives. We cannot erase the harm we have caused ourselves and others. But, with vigilance, we can become strong enough and wise enough to avoid our past mistakes, learn to make decisions that are in our best interest, and find happiness.

Reflections

_____

_____

_____

_____

_____

_____

_____

_____

_____

_____

_____

_____

_____

_____

_____

_____

_____

_____

_____

_____

What changes do you want to make?

_____

_____

_____

_____

_____

_____

_____

What steps do you need to take to bring about change?

_____

_____

_____

_____

_____

_____

_____

_____

_____

_____

*"Expectations always lead to disappointments.
Let's try to expect less and then in return we'll
see that we receive so much more."*

— Rahul Singh

3. UNMET EXPECTATIONS

What Therapy Teaches Us

We are all imperfect, and we all live flawed lives. We all know that living daily life can be challenging, and some days, we don't understand why things aren't going as planned. "If others would only behave how I think they should. Don't they see things the way I do? Don't they know that I know best, and they only need to comply with my wishes to create a perfect world?" Yeah, right! We see that our family, co-workers, and the rest of the world do not meet our expectations, and we are left expending valuable emotional energy in frustration and anger. "Why am I unhappy?"

I began seeing a therapist years ago to find my way to a happier life. The root of my unhappiness eventually became apparent. I learned and started to believe that the world is exactly how it's supposed to be. In therapy, I realized that "unhappiness lives in unmet expectations." When I looked at my life, it became clear that my expectations of things outside of myself, especially the behaviors of others, were the core of my unhappiness.

21

Finding Happiness

To find happiness, you must change your ways of seeing and your attitudes toward the world. If I did not accept the world just as it was supposed to be, I would remain frustrated and unhappy forever. The rest of the world, I learned, did not want to comply with my perfectionistic plans.

Unhappiness lives in unmet expectations. To find happiness, you must change your perspective and attitude toward the world.

Life is sometimes unfair. But when you see reality clearly and accept it just as it is, peace and serenity can take hold. Acceptance allows you to stop fighting with the truth and being unhappy. Fighting against 'what is' leads only to frustration and never a peaceful resolution. You can expend your energy in anger and outrage or accept life on life's terms and move toward greater happiness and life satisfaction.

Acceptance

In the Alcoholics Anonymous Big Book, a member shares:

"And acceptance is the answer to all my problems today. When I am disturbed, it is because I find some person, place, thing, or situation 'some fact of my life' unacceptable to me, and I can find no serenity until I accept that person, place, thing, or situation as being exactly the way it is supposed to be at this moment." We are free to be who we are when we believe this.

22

When you shed expectations, your whole understanding of yourself and the world shift. You see the world, other people, and yourself in a new way.

I tell those I work with that each day is like a pie. The pie only has so many pieces, and I ask, 'How much of today's pie do you want to waste on resentment and anger?' The answer is almost always 'none.' Time spent on expectations is very often a waste of energy. I explain: "We only have so much energy each day. Sitting in anger and resentment is a waste of energy."

You can sit in anger and shake your fist at the world's unfairness, or you can work on acceptance. This is seeing and accepting reality as it is, not as you wish it to be. Most of us feel disappointed when life does not go as planned, but spending energy sitting in disappointment makes little sense. How much of today's pie do you want to devote to acceptance, growth, flexibility, and contentment?

Decide: you can expend your energy on life events that you cannot change, or you can begin to accept life as it is and focus your energy on the positive. But, again, unhappiness lives in unmet expectations. So, whether you are disappointed in your partner, yourself, or the world, you must consciously decide which direction to go.

Ask: "What is in my best interest?" Is it to sit with a negative, ungrateful attitude, or do you change your perspective and be grateful for what you have and what is within your control? If you choose the latter, you can begin to improve your life.

Change requires focus, commitment, and an open mind. To change your life, you must use mindfulness. This is being aware of your world from moment to moment. Use your inner strength and common sense to accept difficult realities. Be accepting of yourself, of others, and the world.

Reflections

_____

_____

_____

_____

_____

_____

_____

_____

_____

_____

_____

_____

_____

_____

_____

_____

_____

_____

_____

_____

What changes do you want to make?

_____

_____

_____

_____

_____

_____

What steps do you need to take to bring about change?

_____

_____

_____

_____

_____

_____

_____

_____

"Most of our assumptions have outlived their uselessness."

— Marshall McLuhan

4. Mind-Reading

Knowing, Not Guessing, About What's Going On

Do you see reality as it is? Or do you see reality as it is not? Sometimes *how we see is different from what is.* This means that what you see and believe about yourself and your past may not be as you think. This also means that what you see today is not actual reality but reality as uniquely seen and understood through your own eyes.

This clouded way of thinking is directly related to your childhood experiences, past adult experiences, and how your life is now. They all affect how you see and understand the world.

Because you have a clouded view of reality, you don't see your past and present as they are. This is important because it directly affects your relationships. Your clouded view can lead you to what is called *mind-reading.* This is when you believe you know something but have no evidence to support your belief. A good example is thinking you know how someone thinks or feels without evidence supporting your beliefs. When you mind-read, you fill in the blanks about what may or may not be true. This is when your clouded view of reality leads you astray. You make assumptions about how people feel and think about you, but what you believe to be true may not be. Mind-reading occurs when you have expectations of others - such as your spouse - that don't get met. You expect them to understand your needs and wants even though you have not told them what they are.

Sometimes we mind-read - believing that we know for certain how things are - when the facts don't support our beliefs.

When you fall into mind-reading, you make guesses based on limited information and your biases. The emotions you feel aren't t based on fact, and you behave in ways driven by faulty thinking. This leads to dysfunctional behaviors.

Evidence

We all make educated guesses based on non-verbal cues and context, but this process is imperfect. Others' thoughts and emotions vary, making it impossible to accurately determine someone's inner state without asking.

Relying on assumptions and mind-reading can also hinder communication and problem-solving. It is crucial to ask questions and use active listening to avoid misunderstandings and ensure you understand what is happening.

Take a moment to consider what it's like to live a life based on a clouded understanding of reality. How can you choose your life path if you don't see things as they are? Is there enough evidence to support a negative belief, or is your belief unsupported and based on mind-reading and assumption? You cannot know how another person thinks and feels, so when you mind-read, you believe things that aren't real.

How It Looks

An excellent example of mind-reading can be found in your relationship. Sometimes you become upset with your partner because they did not do something you expected them to do. "Why didn't he offer to pick me up from work? Doesn't he care about me?" You are mind-reading, expecting your partner to know what you need or want without telling them. Perhaps your partner didn't see or understand that this is what you wanted. I tell people to open their mouths and ask for what they need and want, regardless of how much they believe their partner "should know" without them having to ask. When you don't, you will find yourself disappointed over and over again.

Let's use work as another example. One of my clients got fired last week. His boss did not explain why, and he didn't ask. Instead, he started mind-reading. He blamed himself, convinced that he must have done something wrong. He could not find a new job immediately, so negative core beliefs such as "I am a failure" and "I am not enough" led to depression. In turn, it was increasingly difficult for him to find a new job as his depression affected his ability to motivate himself.

He believed he was a failure, unable to hold a job and care for his family. He had lost his self-confidence and was unable to move forward. I asked, "Other than this experience, what facts support your belief that you are a failure and unable to find another job?" His mind-reading about why he was fired led to shame and despair, as he believed he was a failure, and something he did or lacked led him to be fired.

Let's go back to the beginning of this example: last week, one of my clients was fired. His boss did not explain why, and he didn't ask. Now, let's widen our perspective. Instead of mind-reading, let's re-examine what occurred and consider other possibilities.

Mind-reading may be leading you to believe things that aren't true. In relationships, stop assuming your partner knows what you need and want and start asking for it.

"I don't know why I was fired." Maybe you weren't doing a good job, and that's the reason. But, if you know you were doing a good job, there are other possibilities to consider. You may have been doing a good job, but your boss didn't really like you personally, so he decided to get rid of you. It's also possible that you were fired because the company could no longer afford to keep you on and is planning to hire someone with less experience at a reduced salary. Nothing was wrong with your work, but your boss didn't want to pay you. It's even plausible that the boss' son was looking for a job, and he replaced you with him. Again, there was nothing wrong with you. Circumstances led to you being fired.

There are many explanations as to why this happened. Mind-reading convinced my client that he was fired because he wasn't good enough, and it was his fault. But, one of the alternative explanations may have been the real reason. Don't assume it must be your fault when something goes wrong. Mind-reading can lead to negative core beliefs not based on facts.

Reality

Challenge yourself to see reality as it is and not what you assume it to be. Mind-reading may be leading you to believe things that aren't true. In relationships, stop assuming your partner knows what you need and want and start asking for it. Look at the evidence and see reality for what it is, not what you think it is. Challenge your thoughts and assumptions. Ask yourself, "Am I mind-reading?"

The evidence rarely lies, while mind-reading sometimes does. Seeing the world, others, and yourself more clearly will allow you to make positive life changes. You must know who you truly are to grow and create positive changes in your life. Mind-reading makes you believe things that aren't true, can deepen negative core beliefs, and keep you from living the life you want to live.

Reflections

_____

_____

_____

_____

_____

_____

_____

_____

_____

_____

_____

_____

_____

_____

_____

_____

_____

_____

_____

_____

_____

What changes do you want to make?

_____

_____

_____

_____

_____

_____

_____

What steps do you need to take to bring about change?

_____

_____

_____

_____

_____

_____

_____

_____

_____

_____

"All people cross the line from childhood to adulthood with a secondhand opinion of who they are. Without any questioning, we take as truth whatever our parents and other influentials have said about us during our childhood, whether these messages are communicated verbally, physically, or silently."

— *Heyward Ewart*

5. EXAMINING CORE BELIEFS

Challenging How You See Yourself

Take a moment to think about what you believe about yourself. Who are you? Are you a good person? Do you think you are a failure? Do you feel you aren't good enough? Do you believe you are lovable? Do you think you are valuable?

These are examples of 'core beliefs' - what you believe about yourself deep down. Your core beliefs are with you every moment of every day. Even though you may not be aware of them, they are there. And your core beliefs directly impact your thoughts, feelings, and behaviors. Positive core beliefs support self-worth and esteem. But negative core beliefs poison your daily life and keep you from building and maintaining positive self-worth and esteem.

Negative Core Beliefs

Many of my clients reveal that one of their strongest core beliefs is that they are a failure. Because core beliefs cloud and distort people's thinking, they say, "I was a failure yesterday, I am a failure today, and I will be a failure tomorrow. I feel stuck and unhappy."

We were not born with negative beliefs about ourselves. We internalize and accept that these beliefs are true because, at some point in our life, someone told us they were true, and we believed them.

If you began believing this as a child, the days, weeks, months, and years pass, and the negative core belief that you are a failure becomes deeply ingrained. You can no longer remember when you started believing you were a failure, but now, deep down, this belief is an absolute truth.

Eventually, no matter how well you've hidden this belief inside of yourself, it sometimes activates and enters your consciousness. When this happens, negative thinking and self-talk start. For example, you may feel intense shame when someone criticizes you. When this happens, it can feel like negative emotions are flooding your brain.

To lower the intensity of your shame, you must first be aware of the feeling when it comes up. If you don't know what you are feeling is shame, you can do nothing to change it. Recognizing your emotions requires 'mindfulness,' having the ability to recognize and name your feelings as they arise. If you know you are feeling shame, you can do something about it.

Is a negative core belief 'pushing' your emotional reaction and making it more intense? What negative core belief is it? Use insight to attack negative feelings. What is insight? Insight is your understanding of why you are feeling how you are feeling. Here, the negative core belief "I am a failure " may have activated your shame." Refocus on your positive core beliefs to challenge this negative one and *fight off* this belief by challenging its validity. Are you a failure? And, why do you believe this? Understanding why a negative core belief was activated is *having insight* into the problem. Negative core beliefs form as the result of past experiences. Having this insight helps you understand why you are feeling the way you are and makes it easier to shift away from negative emotions when they come up.

Being Triggered

Negative core beliefs make you overreact. Problems become amplified because your negative core beliefs have been activated. If a current problem is this big:

|—|

And your negative core beliefs add this level of intensity to your reaction:

|———|, then your reaction will be:

|—| plus |———|, or

|—————|, an overreaction.

You can occasionally be triggered by things you have already resolved in therapy. When you work through past trauma, it can heal, but it does leave a scar you still carry inside. Sometimes the scar gets irritated, and a negative core belief gets activated. So, even though you have healed, you can still be triggered by past trauma.

Believing that you're a failure or not good enough can bring up feelings of fear and anxiety. Have you ever felt highly anxious without knowing why? Reflect on whether these feelings result from a negative core belief activation. We sometimes feel emotional without knowing why. These feelings may be the result of negative core belief activation.

When you are mindful, you can use insight to question your thinking, change your emotions, and choose your behaviors. You act instead of react.

How Negative Core Beliefs Cloud Your Thinking

Your thoughts lead to your emotions, and your emotions drive your behaviors. I add that your core beliefs cloud your thinking, making your emotions more intense (bigger) than expected in response to certain situations. When a negative core belief is activated and clouds your thinking, your emotional intensity level increases, leading to behavior that would be considered an overreaction. How this looks: your core beliefs cloud your thoughts, your thoughts lead to your emotions, and your emotions drive your behavior. Clouded thoughts lead to an inaccurate emotional response, and that response drives dysfunctional behaviors.

When you become aware of a negative thought or emotion, question whether negative core beliefs have clouded it. Most, if not all, of your negative core beliefs, are baseless, untrue, or can be changed. Work to recognize when negative core beliefs affect your thoughts and emotions and question whether the belief is true. This will help clear your thinking and lessen the intensity of or change your emotional response. This awareness can be life-changing. Instead of reacting to things, you can choose how to behave. Being mindful allows you to recognize and question your self-talk. Doing this helps lessen the intensity of emotional reactions. This will enable you to choose how to act and not fall victim to reacting and behaving in dysfunctional ways.

Your core beliefs cloud your thoughts, your thoughts lead to your emotions, and your emotions drive your behavior. Clouded thoughts lead to an inaccurate emotional response, and that response drives dysfunctional behaviors.

Healthy Core Beliefs

Core beliefs aren't just negative. A healthy core belief might be "I am a good, kind person," or "I accept myself fully," or "I am human, and sometimes I make mistakes." These core beliefs reflect positively on yourself while recognizing human imperfection and the need to be kind to yourself when you make a mistake. Note that perfectionistic self-expectations aren't activated due to your positive core beliefs. Expecting yourself to be perfect is a trap because when you aren't perfect, you reinforce negative core beliefs like "I am a failure."

If you believe you are a failure at your core, you neglect your humanness and the importance of self-forgiveness. If you expect to be perfect, you are doomed to a life of disappointment and self-loathing. It is near impossible to experience appropriate levels of self-esteem when you expect yourself to be perfect.

When negative core beliefs form, they 're-wire' your brain. But this can be fixed. This is why challenging your negative core belief systems is crucial.

Internalizing the Negative

Take a moment to reflect on a newborn. A child enters our world completely innocent. No child is born a "failure," and no child is "just not good enough." All babies are inherently good and completely free of negative beliefs about themselves. Therefore, realize that you were not born with negative beliefs about yourself. Others handed you these beliefs. But they are not yours. You internalized and accepted that what others said was true. You believe your negative core beliefs to be true because someone told you they were true at some point in your life, and you believed them.

Growing up, you also form negative core beliefs by comparing yourself to others. I remember how early these comparisons began. In elementary school, I was taught that I was not the smartest kid in the class. Was I dumb? Part of me started to believe this. Then I discovered that I wasn't the best athlete. Am I expected to be a great athlete? Am I 'enough?'

When confronting negative core beliefs, it is essential to reflect on childhood. Recall anxious experiences like waiting to be picked by a team at recess. If you were good, you'd be chosen quickly. But if you were terrible, you'd be picked last. Some of us were also teased, sometimes relentlessly. As adults, we may discover that our negative core beliefs were formed then. Why would you carry core beliefs internalized as a child when you are an adult? Consider whether you would believe something mean a child said to you today. Probably not. But childhood experiences like being teased can haunt you and perpetuate negative belief systems. To help change your negative core beliefs, you must recognize that *just because someone said something doesn't mean it's true.* Use insight as your tool to challenge and change your negative core beliefs.

Confront The Negative

To build self-worth, it is essential to confront your negative core beliefs. Reflect and discover who or what experience taught you beliefs like you weren't good enough. Revisit shameful experiences from your youth and recognize that children have nothing to be ashamed of. Shame shouldn't be carried for a lifetime. Instead, you must learn from it and make changes.

You can't change the past, but you can change how you see the past. Changing your perspective on the past brings a new understanding and allows you to question whether your negative core beliefs are true. When you do this, you will discover that many of your negative core beliefs aren't yours - they belong to someone else - someone who shamed you into believing they were true.

Stop comparing yourself to others. Comparisons aren't worth your energy. Work to accept and cherish who you are. Be proud of who you are, challenge your negative core beliefs, and accept yourself fully.

Reflections

What changes do you want to make?

_____

_____

_____

_____

_____

_____

_____

What steps do you need to take to bring about change?

_____

_____

_____

_____

_____

_____

_____

_____

_____

"Resentment is like drinking poison and waiting for the other person to die."

— St. Augustine

"Anger, resentment, and jealousy don't change the heart of others - it only changes yours."

— Shannon Alder

6. LET GO OF RESENTMENTS

Stop Depleting Your Energy

Growth and change cannot be achieved without energy. Life stands still without it. Each day you have a finite amount of energy to live your daily life. It is essential to keep your energy from being drained and depleted.

Without energy, your goals cannot be met, your life cannot improve, and your potential will remain unrealized. All change depends on energy. To be your best self and live the life you envision requires having enough energy to keep moving in the direction you choose.

Holding resentments is one of the most significant cognitive and emotional drains on your limited daily energy. Resentment is a powerful and all-consuming emotion arising from injustice, anger, and bitterness. We all experience resentment, but holding onto them can have significant negative impacts on your emotional well-being, relationships, and personal growth.

The Problem

We have all experienced past injustices and negative encounters that have resulted in resentment. Yet, we tend to hold on to resentments even though they are damaging and painful.

Resentments take a toll on your emotional well-being in various ways. They bring up negative emotions such as anger, bitterness, and hostility. Research shows that these negative feelings perpetuate constant anxiety and can lead to chronic stress and depression.

One of the most significant consequences of holding onto resentments is the strain it puts on your relationships. Resentments lead to relationship problems, misunderstandings, and communication problems. It is near impossible to have healthy relationships when negative emotions consume you.

Holding resentments may seem justified, but doing so depletes your energy as you try to sustain the anger and frustration that accompany it. St. Augustine wisely wrote that having a resentment is like drinking poison and waiting for the other person to die. You hurt yourself while the target of your resentment remains unaffected.

Resentments also lead you to lose control of your life. You may find yourself unable to regulate your emotions, and you can become overcome by uncomfortable, painful feelings. Helpless to take control, you become preoccupied with the injustice that led to your resentment. But past transgressions cannot be undone, so there can be no fair resolution.

You must strive to be your best self, to grow and change, and to move continuously toward fulfillment and happiness. This goal is impossible to reach if feelings of resentment remain a part of your life.

Resentments can also hinder your personal growth. When you hold resentments, you remain stuck in the past. The negative energy associated with resentment drains your mental and emotional resources and prevents you from focusing on your personal growth and potential. You can focus on living a more positive and fulfilling life by letting go of resentments.

Justified anger usually distorts cognition, and you may fail to recognize the powerless feelings that holding a resentment causes. There is nothing that can be done to make things right. Resentments waste energy that could have been used for positive life changes.

Life Choices

How you live your life is a choice. You can choose a life of resentment, unhappiness, and anger - or a life of abundance, fulfillment, and peace. You have no control over the behavior of others. When you attach yourself to the belief that you can control others – when you live a life of codependence – your ability to live the life you desire becomes impossible. Your resentments make you powerless over your own life. Your feelings and behaviors become dictated by it. The memory of the unjust behavior now controls your life choices.

Letting Go

Letting go and forgiving others can be a difficult task. But, to live a happy life, you must accept that resentments are self-injurious and must be avoided altogether. Forgiveness is often difficult. If you can't find forgiveness, focus on acceptance. When you forgive, accept injustice, and let it go, you are performing an act of self-care.

To be happy, you must let injustice and unfairness slip into the past. The past is gone, the present defines your life, and the future presents opportunities to live your chosen life. To grow and live the life you deserve, forgiving and accepting what others have done is essential. You must also forgive yourself for the pain you caused yourself by holding a resentment.

One of the most compelling reasons to let go of resentments is to find peace of mind and free yourself of negative emotions. Holding onto resentments consumes your thoughts, drains your energy, and prevents you from being mindful and living in the present. Letting go allows you to find inner peace. It allows you to focus on the positive and be grateful for the world surrounding you.

Life is a gift. And having been given this gift, you have an obligation – a responsibility – to live a whole and meaningful life. You must strive to be your best self, to grow and change, and to move continuously toward fulfillment and happiness. This goal is impossible to reach if feelings of resentment remain.

Never forget the importance of living a full life and being present in the lives of those you love. This can only be accomplished if you let go of your justified anger and stop living a life consumed by anger and resentment. Let your resentments go so you can live a life of contentment and happiness.

Reflections

_____

_____

_____

_____

_____

_____

_____

_____

_____

_____

_____

_____

_____

_____

_____

_____

_____

_____

_____

_____

_____

What changes do you want to make?

_____

_____

_____

_____

_____

_____

_____

What steps do you need to take to bring about change?

_____

_____

_____

_____

_____

_____

_____

_____

_____

"Admitting one's own faults is the first step to changing them, and it is a demonstration of true bravery and integrity."

— Philip Johnson

7. PERSONAL VALUES

What Are Your Morals and Values?

To live the life you desire, it is important to take an inventory of your morals and values. Living in congruence with them allows you to minimize feelings of guilt and shame, and your negative core beliefs have an opportunity to remain quiet.

If you are not living your life with integrity and behaving by your morals and values, you will experience unhappiness, anxiety, and discontent. Completing an inventory of what you believe your morals and values are is a crucial step on your road to happiness and contentment. Take the time to uncover what you believe in and consider how this impacts your decision-making and how you live your life.

Your morals and values directly impact your behavior, decisions, and relationships. They are crucial in shaping your character and determining your life direction.

Being Who You Really Are

Living in alignment with your morals and values allows you to be true to yourself. Take a moment to think about whether the choices and actions you take each day reflect your beliefs. If not, why? Asking this question will help you understand who you are at your core. With this knowledge, you can identify and do what is most important in your life. It can lead to experiencing a sense of authenticity and inner harmony. Living by your morals and values supports positive self-worth, and when you prioritize and honor your morals and values, you cultivate a genuine sense of purpose and fulfillment. Most of us seek to improve our understanding of who we are, clarify what we believe in, and decide what changes we must make to live a better life.

Living by your morals and values supports positive self-worth. When you prioritize and honor your morals and values, you cultivate a genuine sense of purpose and fulfillment.

Finding Your Purpose

Living by your morals and values allows you to find your sense of purpose. They help you understand the world and your role in it. When you live by your values, you feel your actions have greater significance and contribute to something beyond yourself. This sense of purpose and meaning enhances your overall well-being and creates a solid sense of positive self-worth.

The Impact On Your Life Direction

Understanding your morals and values will help guide important life choices. When faced with difficult decisions, your values provide a moral framework that enables you to make choices aligned with your core principles. This leads to a greater sense of confidence in the choices you make.

Living by your morals and values increases your feelings of positive self-esteem and confidence. It also strengthens your relationships because others understand you more clearly. Over time, living a life of integrity - driven by your values - leads to sustainable personal power and control over your life. This helps you to successfully find what it is you seek each day.

Integrity Defined

When you live in a way that is true to your core values, you live with integrity. When you live with integrity, you are living your life in congruence with your morals and values. Integrity increases and maintains the depth of your self-worth, solidifies your self-confidence, and provides you with inner strength. Having integrity is almost tangible, as people can feel it when they are around you. It is solid ground on which to live.

There are life circumstances that are out of your control, such as the behavior of others. Regardless of how others behave, it is important to live according to your values and interact with others in a way you believe to be right. Strength of conviction, belief in yourself, and an unwavering alignment between your values and actions are the foundation of integrity. This allows you to focus on your life goals without being deterred and helps you to achieve them successfully.

Complete a 'Values' Inventory

Taking a 'values' inventory seems straightforward, but it does require some personal reflection and even some pain. To do this inventory, sit down and write out a list of your core values. You may value being kind to others, speaking up when you disagree, having a lifelong commitment to a partner, and not letting others down when they need help. You may value honesty and taking care of your family.

While completing your inventory, ask yourself if you have lived by these values over your lifetime. For example, have you cheated on a partner in the past? Have you been unkind to others? Have you been unreliable when others have asked for help? The values inventory serves three purposes: 1) to identify what you value in concrete terms, 2) to identify the times when you fell short of living up to them, and 3) to understand why you fell short and how to correct it.

When you complete your inventory, be careful with perfectionism. Your goal is not to be perfect. This inventory will help you be more mindful and aware of your beliefs. It allows you to reflect on how you've behaved in the past and helps you decide what to change about yourself and how you behave.

When you know who you are and what you believe, you can use mindfulness (awareness) to help you live by your morals and values. Without being mindful, you won't be able to change your thinking or behaviors when they don't match up with your morals and values. Mindfulness allows you to recognize your thinking and behavior and make necessary changes.

Oddly, your values inventory may identify some conflicting values. To live in congruence with one value, it may be difficult to also live by another. Therefore, it is essential to prioritize your values and think hard about the consequences of not being able to live by one value over another. Trust your instincts and do what you think is right, even under difficult circumstances.

Falling Short

The final part of completing your values inventory is to examine how you've fallen short throughout your life. Consider the vast number of bad choices and mistakes you've made. Don't get too caught up in the small stuff. In this step, you should focus on apparent transgressions.

Healthy shame is when you recognize what you must change about yourself and take action to make those changes.

As painful as it may be, look closely at past behaviors and identify ones that you still think about and regret. I am talking about the memories that keep you up at night. Recalling these memories may bring up feelings of guilt and shame. However, doing this has an important purpose. When recalling these memories, you will easily identify your morals and values because you know you will never act like that again. What were the morals and values you betrayed in those moments? Add these to your values inventory.

When feelings of guilt and shame arise during this process, understand that toxic guilt and shame are when you carry feelings of guilt and shame about something throughout your life. Over time, toxic guilt and shame poison you. These emotions, if not resolved, tend to eat you up inside. Healthy guilt is when you learn from your bad behavior and use that knowledge to ensure that you never behave like that again. You learn from past mistakes and work on shedding the guilt and shame associated with them. You heal from it and move forward in a healthy way. Shame is feeling bad about who you are. To resolve it, you need to make healthy changes. If you don't, you will carry feelings of shame with you forever. Healthy shame is when you recognize what you must change about yourself and take action to make those changes. It is healthy to let guilt and shame motivate you to make fewer mistakes and live according to your morals and values.

What can you do with the shame and guilt that comes up? Feeling these emotions can be paralyzing. But, they have a clear purpose: to help you change. Knowing what triggers these emotions is essential. This guides you and helps you to avoid repeating the same mistakes. They help you identify what you need to change about yourself.

Identify Your Flaws

The time has come to face reality. To bring about permanent life change, you must take a gut-wrenching look at the character flaws that lead to your past failings. If not checked, these flaws can hurt those around you and will continue reinforcing your negative core beliefs. When your negative core beliefs are reinforced, your self-worth and self-esteem decrease. To build self-worth and self-esteem, these flaws must be identified and fixed.

What do I mean by 'flaws?' Here, I am referring to what motivated your bad behavior or any behavior you are not proud of. For example, were you motivated by pride when you were unkind? Or were you motivated by greed when you took advantage of someone? Or envy? Did you assassinate someone's character to feel better about yourself? Take a step back, reflect, and identify the flaws that drove your bad behavior. These flaws are the reason so many of us fail ourselves and others. They are a large part of why you are not living a life of contentment and happiness.

Live The Life You Choose

As a therapist and life coach, my job is to guide people toward the life they most desire and help them do the work necessary to get there. To arrive, you must live by your morals and values. To do otherwise is to betray yourself and be unable to live the life you want to live. To live a life that is true to your morals and values is to live with integrity. When you live with integrity, you are living a life that is true to who you are.

Reflections

_____

_____

_____

_____

_____

_____

_____

_____

_____

_____

_____

_____

_____

_____

_____

_____

_____

_____

_____

_____

_____

_____

What changes do you want to make?

_____

_____

_____

_____

_____

_____

_____

What steps do you need to take to bring about change?

_____

_____

_____

_____

_____

_____

_____

_____

_____

"For many, negative thinking is a habit which, over time, becomes an addiction."

— Peter McWilliams

8. NEGATIVE THINKING

Identify Your Thoughts and Emotions

Reflect for a moment on how you think. You will discover two things when you distill your thoughts to the basics. The first, positive thoughts, contribute to self-esteem and an overall sense of well-being. You view yourself, those around you, and the world in a positive way. The second, negative thoughts, lead to low self-worth and over-generalizations about how bad your life is. Most of us want a life that brings more positives than negatives. But how do you achieve this goal?

An essential step in minimizing negative thoughts is having the ability to recognize your thoughts and emotions in the moment. This is called being mindful. When you start to identify what you are thinking and feeling in the moment, you can begin to understand why you have negative thoughts and work to change them.

Thinking and then having an emotional reaction happens almost instantaneously. As your thoughts lead to your emotions, I see thoughts and emotions as two sides of the same coin.

Sometimes you recognize your thoughts first, but sometimes you recognize your feelings first.

If you begin to recognize your thoughts and emotions, you can choose your behaviors. Doing this can change your entire life.

Being mindful and aware of your emotions is critical to lowering their intensity and changing them. If you recognize how you feel, you can examine why you feel a certain way. When you do this, the intensity of the emotion lessens. To help you recognize your emotions, author Pia Mellody has broken them down into eight basic feelings:

1. Anger (resentment, irritation, and frustration)

2. Fear (apprehension, overwhelmed, threatened)

3. Pain (hurt, pity, sad, lonely)

4. Joy (happy, elated, hopeful)

5. Passion (enthusiasm, desire, zest)

6. Love (affection, tenderness, compassion, warmth)

7. Shame (embarrassment, humble, exposed)

8. Guilt (regretful, contrite, remorseful)

I recommend the following exercise to help you with emotional recognition. First, keep a list of the eight emotions on your smartphone. Next, set the alarm on your smartphone to go off every half hour. Then, when the alarm rings, go over the emotions list and identify how you feel at that moment. After doing this for a few days, your ability to recognize your emotions should improve. I've done this, and it helps.

What is the Cognitive Model?

The cognitive model posits that your thoughts lead to your emotions, and your emotions lead to your behaviors. This occurs in order, but as mentioned, you will often recognize your emotions before knowing the thoughts that led to them. So, being mindful of and recognizing your feelings can be the first step toward identifying your thoughts, changing them, and deciding how to behave.

Anger is an excellent example of an emotion that is easy to recognize. When you are angry, your body has a recognizable reaction. When you begin to feel anger, you will notice heat rising in your chest, and your face will flush. To help you lower the intensity of your anger or let it go altogether, pause for a moment and recognize the thoughts that led to your anger. This is being mindful. If you don't know what you are feeling, you can do nothing to change it.

A good example is getting angry when you are in a waiting room and you wait and wait to see your doctor (never me, of course!) You had a 3 o'clock appointment, and it's now 4 o'clock. You feel anger rising in your chest and think, "What a jerk. This doctor has no respect for me." Think about what came first, your thoughts about being disrespected, or your feelings of anger. Recognizing your thoughts and emotions allows you to then choose your behaviors. Should you go to the front desk and begin yelling, or should you go to the front desk and calmly remind them of your appointment and ask for an update? This is when I suggest you 'add a pause' to allow you to recognize your thoughts and emotions before you act.

When you recognize angry feelings and associated thoughts, ask yourself if your anger is helpful at that moment or if it depletes your energy and detracts from happiness. Which direction do you want to go? If you decide that angry feelings are not adding anything positive to your life and that these feelings may lead to negative behaviors (yelling at the office staff), think things through and allow your angry feelings to dissipate.

Identifying your thoughts and emotions allows you to choose how to behave and not just react to feelings that arise. *If you begin to recognize your thoughts and emotions, you can choose your behaviors. Doing this can change your entire life.* I have used anger as an example, but this applies to other 'negative' emotions such as fear, shame, and guilt.

The Role of Perspective

What can you do to change negative thoughts? Cognitive theory teaches us to reframe the problem, consider all possibilities, and see problems from different perspectives. In the doctor's office example, consider whether the doctor is doing something to you personally when he runs late. Probably not. Some doctors run late because some patients' health problems require more time to address than the doctor allows. It's also possible that the doctor forgot to pay his electric bill and is frantically calling the electric company to avoid having the power shut off! We don't know why he's late, so why let anger waste your limited daily energy?

When you widen your perspective, you can avoid negative thinking and emotions. If you reframe and consider your situation from a different perspective, you may realize that your emotions aren't based on facts. In this example, an alternate thought might be, "Medical appointments can be so frustrating. But I am here to take care of my health, and having good health is one of the most important things in life. Even though I'm frustrated, I'm taking care of myself." When you widen your perspective, you lessen the intensity of, change, or avoid negative thoughts and emotions.

One of the most important things I've learned is that ***events are neutral***. You add meaning to them. Remember that most of what is outside of yourself is out of your control. You can react to adverse life events with anger or fear, widen your perspective, and avoid negative thoughts and emotions. You only have a certain amount of emotional energy each day; more often than not, your negative thoughts and emotions are just a waste of your energy. You determine how life events affect you.

Nobody's perfect, and you will struggle to accept life on life's terms. Even though your thoughts may be negative sometimes, try to be mindful and aware. Recognize your emotions, uncover the thoughts that led to your emotions, work to change your perspective, and choose how to behave. Change your life by choosing to act and not react. As a result, you will begin experiencing more positive emotions, and your life will change dramatically.

Reflections

_____

_____

_____

_____

_____

_____

_____

_____

_____

_____

_____

_____

_____

_____

_____

_____

_____

_____

_____

_____

_____

_____

What changes do you want to make?

_____

_____

_____

_____

_____

_____

_____

What steps do you need to take to bring about change?

_____

_____

_____

_____

_____

_____

_____

_____

_____

"We cannot solve our problems with the same thinking we used when we created them."

— Albert Einstein

9. COGNITIVE DISTORTIONS

The Impact of Negative Thinking

As a therapist and life coach, talking with my clients about thinking errors or 'cognitive distortions' is gratifying. Pointing out a thinking error, and having someone see and understand the error is often a moment when significant change occurs.

Cognitive distortions are ways of thinking that skew your perception of reality and influence your emotions and behaviors. These distortions can lead to negative thinking and affect your ability to make rational choices.

Cognitive distortions lead you to misunderstand reality. How can that be possible? Reality is reality, after all. But how you see and understand reality is based on your perspective.

These distortions have a profound impact on your mental health. Distorted thinking, such as black-and-white thinking, catastrophizing, and overgeneralization, contribute to negative emotions like depression and anxiety. They can also lead to feelings of low self-worth. Cognitive distortions reinforce negative core beliefs and create a clouded view of yourself and the world.

Your relationships can be affected as thinking errors lead to misinterpretations, assumptions, and negative judgments about the intentions of others. This can lead to conflicts and misunderstandings. Cognitive distortions lead to ineffective communication and difficulty understanding your partner's behaviors.

When you 'mind-read,' you believe someone is thinking something when no facts support your beliefs. This is a thinking error that can lead to negative emotions and relationship problems.

Your ability to make rational decisions is also affected by distorted thinking, as it impacts your judgment and leads to poor decision-making. For instance, ignoring the positive and only focusing on the negative can lead to an overly pessimistic outlook on life. Cognitive distortions can also prevent you from considering alternative perspectives when difficulties arise. They can limit your problem-solving abilities.

Cognitive distortions are detrimental to your self-esteem and personal growth. Distorted thinking often involves self-critical and self-defeating thoughts. You may look at yourself one way, for example, 'I am stupid,' when this is untrue. These thinking errors reinforce negative core beliefs and undermine your confidence, motivation, and belief in yourself. Correcting cognitive distortions is crucial because you can't see the present or the future clearly if you don't. They may have also played a detrimental role in your past.

These distortions have a negative impact on your overall well-being. By distorting your perceptions and generating negative thoughts, cognitive distortions lead to anxiety and difficulty regulating your emotions. Cognitive distortions not only create negativity, but they also impact your physical health and your quality of life.

The 10 Most Common Cognitive Distortions

All-or-Nothing Thinking

You see things in black and white. For example, if you don't do something perfectly, you see yourself as a failure.

Overgeneralization

You see a single adverse event as a never-ending pattern of defeat. "I was passed over for the promotion I expected to get. I'll never get a promotion."

Mental Filter

You pick out a single negative detail and dwell on it exclusively so that your vision of all reality goes black.

Disqualifying the Positive

You reject positive experiences by insisting they "don't count" for some reason. You stay stuck in a negative belief contradicted by your everyday experiences. For example, you receive an award but believe it was a mistake.

Jumping to Conclusions

You make a negative interpretation even though no facts convincingly support your conclusion. This includes a) mind-reading - when you arbitrarily conclude that someone is reacting negatively to you and you don't take the time to investigate if it's true. and b) fortune telling - when you anticipate that things will turn out badly and are convinced that your prediction is already a fact.

Magnification (Catastrophizing) or Minimization

You exaggerate the importance of things ("I missed watching 'The Bachelor' tonight. I think I'm going to die"), or you inappropriately make light of something important ("So I missed your high school graduation. I promise I'll be there when you graduate college.")

Emotional Reasoning

You assume that your negative emotions reflect how things are – "I feel it, so it must be true." An example is when you feel guilty about something someone else has done.

Should Statements

You try to motivate yourself with should and should not statements, not taking responsibility for doing what is expected of you. The emotional consequence is guilt and sometimes shame (I'm no good, I never get anything done).

Labeling and Mislabeling

This is an extreme form of overgeneralization. Instead of recognizing an error, you attach a negative label to yourself: "I'm a loser." When someone else's behavior upsets you, you attach a negative label to them, "He's a jerk." Mislabeling involves describing an event with emotionally loaded language.

Personalization

You see yourself as the cause of some negative external event for which you were not primarily responsible. This includes things like believing you are responsible for a baseball team losing a game because you forgot to watch.

How Cognitive Distortions Impact Daily Life

Cognitive distortions can create chaos and misunderstandings when your feelings are based on something untrue. Here is an example of how "jumping to conclusions" can impact your relationships:

You are taking a college course, and your final exam is the following day. Your partner is out of town and doesn't call to wish you good luck on the exam. You are mad and think he is too busy having fun with friends and forgot about you and the exam. How inconsiderate – he's never there for me.

Being passive-aggressive, you purposely don't call him. Then, after the exam, you get a loving, congratulatory phone call. "Why didn't you call to wish me good luck last night?" "I didn't want to bother you while you were studying. I was so anxious thinking about you that I had trouble sleeping." You had negatively interpreted the situation even though there was no clear evidence to support your conclusion.

Cognitive distortions often occur when you are tired or feeling depressed. In relationships, you can make a mind-reading error, thinking that your partner is thinking something they are not. Ask your partner if what you believe is happening is really happening.

A good example is the last-minute cancellation of a date. You are convinced that an unexpected date night cancellation means your partner no longer cares. But later, you discover that they canceled because their paycheck hadn't been posted yet, and they couldn't afford to go out. Embarrassed at not having money to pay for the date, they canceled, while you thought they didn't want to spend time with you.

The ' fortune telling ' error is another cognitive distortion that can impact your relationships. The 'fortune telling' error is when you believe things will turn out badly without any evidence, and you feel convinced that your prediction is already a fact. For example, before a first date, you convince yourself it won't work out.

Painful Truths

People are often shocked when they discover that something they believed their entire life is untrue. Cognitive distortions can have a devastating impact on a person's life. An example is found in this story a client shared with me. She said she had spent her life believing her father was never proud of her. After her mother's death, she found a letter her father had written to her mother. In it, he went on and on about how talented and unique my client was and how proud he'd been of her.

Reading this changed her life dramatically. She suddenly realized that the deep-seated feelings of shame she had carried with her for years - feelings that began in childhood when she felt she could never live up to her father's expectations – were fiction. This cognitive distortion led to years of personal pain and a struggle with perfectionism. She had lived most of her life with the negative core belief that she wasn't 'good enough.'

This realization affected her deeply. Beliefs she had about herself for years collapsed and left her unsure of what is real and what is not. In therapy, she worked on unraveling the past and healing from the shame she'd felt for so long.

It is natural to make assumptions, but it is hard to build trust if you don't know what is and what is not the truth. As these examples show, cognitive distortions can significantly impact your thoughts, feelings, and how you live your life.

Changing Your View

Cognitive distortions and thinking errors are so common that I help my clients work on them daily. I can't stress enough the importance of correcting them. Remember: thoughts lead to emotions, and emotions lead to behaviors. Thinking errors can lead us to negative feelings when there is nothing to feel negatively about. The result is often dysfunctional behaviors - you behave in a way that is incongruent with reality.

If your thoughts are skewed, your emotional life and subsequent behaviors will be based on a false view of reality. You will misunderstand the behavior of others, and you will not have a clear understanding of yourself and the world around you.

Reflections

_____

_____

_____

_____

_____

_____

_____

_____

_____

_____

_____

_____

_____

_____

_____

_____

_____

_____

_____

_____

_____

_____

_____

What changes do you want to make?

_____

_____

_____

_____

_____

_____

What steps do you need to take to bring about change?

_____

_____

_____

_____

_____

_____

_____

_____

"You are loved just for being who you are, just for existing. You don't have to do anything to earn it. Your shortcomings, your lack of self-esteem, physical perfection, or social and economic success - none of that matters. No one can take this love away from you, and it will always be here."

— *Ram Dass*

10. PERFECTIONISM

Perfection and the Need to Control

Hanging from a nail on a wall and unable to free yourself, you try to be perfect, but you can't get there. Ask yourself why being perfect and in control is so essential. Perfectionists often think, "I am not enough. I must prove my worth," or "I will not be accepted and loved if I am not perfect." Although perfectionism sounds like a positive trait, setting such high standards for yourself can be problematic and negatively affect you, your relationships, and your quality of life.

As a perfectionist, the unattainable standards you set for yourself can create self-criticism, self-doubt, and anxiety. If you're a perfectionist, you may experience high stress and anxiety levels due to the pressure you put on yourself. This leads to depression, substance abuse, and other mental health problems. Your constant fear of failure and judgment can hinder your ability to enjoy personal successes and live a happier, more contented life.

People still hold the core belief that they are what they were told. Just because someone said something doesn't mean it's true.

Growing Up

If the need for perfection and control negatively impacts your life, I believe the place to start looking for reasons why is your childhood. If you grew up being the family "hero," you must be perfect to live up to your parent's expectations. If you faltered, you may have feared that your caregivers would be unhappy with you and that you would not be praised and validated. You would not be loved. To be loved, you had to DO something. You felt you were not loved just for being who you were. To feel loved and safe, perfectionists need to be in control of themselves and their environment. When they are not, anxiety and fear result.

A desire for validation may also stem from not fitting in at school or being teased. Children who experience this quickly learn that being perfect brings the praise and validation they need. "If I am perfect, I will be loved." I have worked with clients who were teased as children, and being teased set the stage for a life of unhappiness. I've discovered that people can still believe they are what they were told as children. If you were teased, it is crucial to reprocess your childhood emotions. Remember: just because someone said something doesn't mean it's true. As an adult, would you believe a 10-year-old who called you a name? In therapy, you can talk about childhood trauma and bring painful memories to the surface.

The Need For Control

To be perfect requires the need for control. Without controlling all aspects of life, including things outside of yourself that cannot be controlled, perfection is out of reach. You may be a great student or great at your job, but getting accepted into the college you want or promoted is out of your control. Be careful not to judge yourself based on external factors you have no control over. This is being co-dependent - judging yourself and allowing your self-worth to be determined by factors outside of yourself that you cannot control. Fear of disapproval, feeling inadequate, and not feeling safe is often at the core of perfectionism and a person's need to control things.

Perfectionism can lead to procrastination and avoidance. Why try if you don't believe you can do something perfectly or better than others? Perfectionists may also take far more time to complete things like homework and work reports. For example, perfectionists may go through many drafts before submitting homework assignments or work reports. Unfortunately, this can lead to unmanageability as they miss deadlines and spend too much time completing them. Perfectionists forget that turning in homework or work reports on time is often just as important as the content of their work.

Perfectionism does not always lead to greater productivity. It can often get in your way. I have worked with people whose perfectionism has immobilized them as they fear making mistakes.

Suffering

Perfectionism can also impede your personal growth and development. The fear of failure and making mistakes may discourage you from trying new things. You may find yourself not participating in activities that may show your weaknesses. This affects your ability to change and grow as a person. Your fear has paralyzed you, and you cannot grow. Perfectionism can also prevent you from learning from your mistakes. You can develop a mindset that resists change out of fear of failure.

In adults, I have seen the need to control create deep depression and high anxiety. I believe that unhappiness lives in unmet expectations. Perfectionism drives the need for greater success, but the outside world is beyond your control. When things do not go as expected, you become depressed and anxious.

You can work on perfectionism and control in psychotherapy. Understanding its origins is the first step, then correcting your beliefs about yourself is the second. Believing you need to be perfect clouds your view of reality and the need to accept the world as it is.

Changing the Way You Think

Therapists often use cognitive therapy to help people overcome perfectionistic behaviors. In cognitive therapy, you are asked to identify your core beliefs about yourself, how they originated, and how they skew your thinking. Clouded thinking can lead to negative emotions. Changing these beliefs requires mindfulness and the ability to identify how you think and feel. But if you are a perfectionist, be careful to avoid perfectionism as you work to resolve these beliefs and emotions.

At birth, we are all perfect. We are free of self-judgment and the negative sense of self-worth that may develop as we grow up. When you can identify when you became a perfectionist and why, you can begin to resolve it and live a more peaceful life.

Reflections

What changes do you want to make?

_____

_____

_____

_____

_____

_____

_____

What steps do you need to take to bring about change?

_____

_____

_____

_____

_____

_____

_____

_____

_____

"Be faithful to that which exists within yourself."

— André Gide

11. CREATING SELF-ESTEEM

Some Basics

When you are alone and things are quiet, take a moment to reflect on how you feel about yourself. Do you feel confident and secure, or are you struggling? If you are struggling, you may be having feelings of low self-esteem. This is when you do not feel happy and content with who you are. To change your perspective on yourself, you must recognize that low self-esteem creates a lack of self-confidence and relationship problems. There are various ways to work on low self-esteem.

Self-esteem refers to your overall evaluation and perception of your worth and value. Self-esteem is crucial in shaping your thoughts, emotions, behaviors, and psychological health.

Self-esteem significantly impacts your mental health and emotional well-being. If you have low self-esteem, your negative thoughts, self-doubt, and feelings of worthlessness seem to circle over and over again with no end in sight. This can contribute to developing mental health problems such as depression, anxiety, and substance abuse. On the other hand, individuals with a healthy level of self-esteem are more resilient in the face of adversity, better equipped to cope with stress and have a greater overall sense of happiness and life satisfaction.

Coping Mechanisms

Self-esteem is a protective factor that is vital in resilience and coping with life's challenges. When you possess a positive self-perception and belief in your abilities, you are more likely to face obstacles with strength. High self-esteem enhances problem-solving skills, promotes a positive mindset, and enables you to bounce back from setbacks, failures, and rejections. It gives you the confidence and inner strength necessary to overcome adversity and navigate life's ups and downs.

Relationships

Self-esteem plays a critical role in establishing and maintaining healthy relationships. When you have a positive self-image and belief in your own worth, you are more likely to communicate better, set effective boundaries, and connect with others in a healthier way. A solid sense of self-esteem enables you to engage in authentic and meaningful relationships because you are more capable of giving and receiving love, support, and acceptance.

Treating Feelings of Low Self-Esteem

Working with a therapist is one of the most effective ways to address and enhance feelings of low self-esteem. This can help identify the root cause of your low self-esteem - when did it start, and what experiences defined it? A therapist provides tools and techniques to work through these issues.

Work with your therapist to uncover when your negative core beliefs began and why you began believing them. Work to change them to positive ones. Doing this will lead to a significant improvement in self-esteem over time.

Cognitive therapy helps combat your negative core beliefs and feelings of low self-worth. It focuses on identifying negative core beliefs and how they influence your thinking and emotions. Negative core beliefs include "I am a failure" or "I am not as smart as other people." To change negative core beliefs and thought patterns, you must attack negative beliefs and question their validity. Are you a failure? Most of the time, you discover that your negative core beliefs are untrue. When you make this discovery, positive core beliefs begin to form, such as "I am a loving and intelligent person."

Replace your negative core beliefs and negative thinking by resolving the origins of these beliefs. Work with your therapist to uncover when your negative core beliefs began and why you began believing them. Then, work to change them to positive ones. Doing this will lead to a significant improvement in self-esteem over time.

Self-Care

Another effective way to treat low self-esteem is through self-care. Doing things that promote self-care can help increase positive feelings of self-esteem and improve overall mental health. Self-care includes doing what you love doing most, like exercising, meditating, listening to music, and seeing friends and family.

Turn to Your Support System

Turning to friends and family almost always helps combat low self-esteem. Talking with someone who loves and supports you can provide emotional support and help reduce feelings of isolation. Don't forget there are also support groups and online communities you can join - these can be helpful as they allow you to connect with others going through similar experiences.

Individuals with a healthy level of self-esteem are more resilient in the face of adversity, better equipped to cope with stress, and have a greater overall sense of happiness and life satisfaction.

The Importance of Goals

Learning new skills and setting goals can also help improve self-esteem. Setting and achieving small goals can give you a sense of accomplishment and improve your self-confidence. In addition, learning new skills or taking on new challenges can provide a sense of personal growth and fulfillment.

You need to practice self-compassion when you are working to change your feelings of low self-esteem. Being kind to yourself and recognizing that everyone has flaws and makes mistakes can help reduce self-criticism and improve self-esteem. Practicing self-compassion can be challenging at first, but it can lead to a more positive self-image and overall well-being.

Treating low self-esteem is a process that requires patience and commitment. You can improve your self-esteem and overall quality of life through therapy, self-care, support from loved ones, setting goals, and practicing self-compassion. Making needed positive changes leads to greater confidence and a change in your beliefs about yourself.

Reflections

_____

_____

_____

_____

_____

_____

_____

_____

_____

_____

_____

_____

_____

_____

_____

_____

_____

_____

_____

_____

_____

_____

What changes do you want to make?

_____

_____

_____

_____

_____

_____

_____

What steps do you need to take to bring about change?

_____

_____

_____

_____

_____

_____

_____

_____

_____

_____

"If you change the way you look at things, the things you look at change."

— Wayne Dyer

12. WORKING WITH A THERAPIST OR LIFE COACH

Learn How to Create Life Changes

When new clients walk through my door, I try to put them at ease. I am as accepting and understanding as I can be. I know that starting therapy can create much anxiety.

Getting in touch with and coming to meet with me is often a challenging, sometimes even painful experience. I understand how difficult it is to start working with a therapist because I felt the same years ago when I started working with one.

If you are reading this, you are likely considering seeing a therapist or life coach. I encourage you to move forward and meet with one. Only then can you decide whether working with a therapist or life coach will help. If you are looking to create life changes, it most likely will.

Now may be the time to work on life goals with a coach, on alleviating depression or anxiety in therapy, or on improving or even saving your relationship by working with your partner in couples therapy or marriage counseling.

Keep in mind that good therapists do not tell you what to do. Instead, they help you identify what you want to work on and then help you with your problem or goal. You may come because you need help with depression, anxiety, or substance abuse or to meet life goals such as finishing a degree, finding a new job, or starting a new business.

We work together to uncover what changes you want to make and which goals you want to meet. You tell me what you've chosen to work on, and I help you to get there. And if you're unsure, we will work together to identify what is important to you and what you want to change or accomplish. If you seek treatment for depression or another mental health struggle, the goal is to lower the intensity of or resolve your emotional struggles. If you have come to work in life coaching, we will focus on meeting life goals.

What Is Therapy and Life Coaching?

As a therapist, I provide psychodynamic psychotherapy and cognitive therapy within what is called a person-centered framework. Using a person-centered framework means that I provide a non-judgmental environment that gives you the freedom to change and grow. I accept you as you are.

Most modern therapeutic methods incorporate person-centered therapy. It creates a supportive therapeutic environment in which empathy, unconditional positive regard, and genuineness are present. This allows you to freely explore your thoughts and feelings and develop a stronger sense of self. I provide a safe and confidential environment for you to openly express your thoughts, emotions, and concerns without fear.

Building a strong therapeutic alliance is crucial. It establishes an empathic and trusting relationship between you and your therapist. The connection or 'fit' between you and your therapist is the most critical element of effective therapy. Counseling encourages you to explore your thoughts, feelings, and experiences and create insight, self-reflection, and a deeper understanding of yourself and your behavior.

The great thing about being an adult is that you can DECIDE to change and work on how to change your life.

Therapists use many different methods to treat people. I provide psychodynamic psychotherapy and cognitive therapy. I use psychodynamic psychotherapy to explore how past experiences and traumas affect your life today. I use cognitive therapy when we focus on identifying and modifying your negative thought patterns and behaviors that contribute to your emotional distress. Cognitive therapy helps you replace clouded beliefs about who you are with more constructive and rational ones, promoting healthier emotions and behaviors.

The Work

Therapy and coaching can assist you in moving forward toward the life you imagine. In a safe, confidential environment, you can speak your truth - no matter what it is or how scared or ashamed you may feel about what you must say. Secrets can make you sick, and in your daily life, your secrets can create problems due to feelings of shame and guilt. They can sabotage your life and poison your relationships.

If you are working on meeting a life goal, life coaching will help you identify what is blocking you from achieving your goal and help you determine what steps you need to take to accomplish it. Sometimes, one of the steps toward achieving a goal in life coaching might be treating and resolving a mental health problem. While working toward your goals in life coaching, you may choose to address a mental health issue in therapy first. For example, if you are feeling depressed or highly anxious, it will be tough to motivate yourself to achieve your life goals without first working on these issues.

The connection or 'fit' between you and your therapist is the most critical element of effective therapy. Counseling encourages you to explore your thoughts, feelings, and experiences and create insight, self-reflection, and a deeper understanding of yourself and your behavior.

If you suffer from a mental health problem such as depression or anxiety, I will help you understand how your feelings may prevent you from meeting your goals. As a therapist, I am a listener, guide, and educator. As a life coach, I help you achieve your life goals and choose your life direction. I help you identify and take the steps you need to take to achieve your goals.

I have witnessed people change their lives dramatically in therapy and life coaching. Together we will work to move you toward greater happiness, contentment, and success. Whether working in psychotherapy or life coaching, committing yourself to change can make it a reality. You would be amazed to see what I have as a therapist and coach. The great thing about being an adult is that you can DECIDE to change and work on how to change your life. Working with a therapist or life coach will help you overcome the obstacles keeping you from emotional health and living the life you want to live.

Reflections

What changes do you want to make?

_____

_____

_____

_____

_____

_____

What steps do you need to take to bring about change?

_____

_____

_____

_____

_____

_____

_____

_____

_____

"Remember, you have been criticizing yourself for years and it hasn't worked. Try approving of yourself and see what happens."

— Louise Hay

13. SELF-JUDGMENT

Why It Happens and How to Fix It

The pain of judging yourself can be debilitating. I have worked with clients who are haunted by almost constant self-judgment. They judge themselves and worry about how others see them. They may wall themselves off as they protect themselves from the judgment of others. As a result, they cannot connect, leaving them feeling alone.

Often, the core belief of people who judge themselves is "I'm not good enough." They feel "less than" other people and may feel like a failure. They struggle to find feelings of self-worth and confidence. The constant echo of self-judgment robs them of living a peaceful, satisfying life. How can you be happy if you rarely feel good about who you are? Working to end self-judgment is essential to build positive self-worth.

We all judge ourselves, but some of us judge ourselves compulsively. Our inner world has become saturated with self-hatred. Self-judgment can result from societal norms, personal beliefs, and core beliefs formed in childhood.

Self-acceptance is the key to lowering the intensity of self-judgment. Accepting yourself and being compassionate toward yourself will help resolve negative self-reflection and judgment.

Societal Norms

Society and our cultural background drives what is considered "normal." Self-judgment can result if you do not feel like you fit in or feel others are judging you because you don't fit in. For example, educational and professional success is considered essential in some cultures. Parents can push children to excel at math or be a great musician. Professional expectations such as "you must be a doctor" can lead to low self-worth if you don't become one. Societal norms regarding sexual orientation can cause those who are not "straight" to feel isolated and judged.

Personal Beliefs

Personal beliefs drive self-judgment. If you believe it is unacceptable to make a mistake, you are setting yourself up for an unhappy life. Mistakes are part of being human and can lead to positive behavior changes. If you are a perfectionist, you will be overly critical of yourself when you cannot meet the standards you have set for yourself.

You may set yourself up for failure if you believe that you are a failure. You may not put sufficient effort into problem-solving, which creates a self-fulfilling prophecy. When you do fail, it reinforces your negative beliefs about yourself and intensifies self-judgment.

Our conscious or subconscious beliefs shape how we perceive ourselves and influence the standards against which we measure our own worth and actions.

Issues In Childhood

Self-judgment can often be the result of a difficult childhood. Negative mirroring by a parent or caregiver can damage your sense of self-worth. As a child, you internalize how your caregivers value you. Children are sponges, and as they don't yet understand self-worth, they internalize the value placed on them from the outside. If you were neglected or abused, you might believe this was what you deserved and are of little value. More subtle messaging is whether you felt like an annoyance or a failure due to being unable to meet expectations. Being compared with a "smarter" sibling is an example. The result may be lifelong self-judgment.

You may have felt rejected because you were not a great student or athlete. Being teased as a child can also drive self-judgment. I have worked with clients who judge themselves as adults due to being teased as children. They carry negative core beliefs formed as a child that still affect them. They continue to chase the love and acceptance they didn't receive when they were young. They try and try, but their need is never satisfied. They try to prove that they are something greater than who they are. Unable to accept themselves for who they are, they live in pain and unhappiness.

You may internalize the expectations others had for you when you were young as your own expectations. You may continue to feel the need to prove yourself. Yet, as an adult, you do not need to please anyone but yourself. You judge yourself for being unable to meet your own standards. You find yourself unhappy as you see it impossible to meet the standards you have set for yourself.

Fighting off Self-Judgement

To effectively let go of self-judgment, you must learn to be compassionate and understanding toward yourself. Use insight and understanding of the problem to help recognize the irrational side of self-judgment. This provides you with the ability to challenge your thinking and emotions. Is what I'm thinking about myself true, or am I judging myself because past experiences are clouding my thinking? Be mindful (aware), and work on acknowledging and changing your thoughts and emotions.

Examine your 'self-talk.' Self-talk is what you say to yourself as you move through your day. Recognize that these thoughts are natural and part of being human. Take a moment to pause, breathe deeply, and be mindful of what is happening within you. By being aware and present, you can challenge your negative self-talk and break free of self-judgment.

When you think negative thoughts about yourself, ask yourself if they are based on facts or assumptions. You can also reframe your thoughts into something positive and realistic. For example, if you make a mistake, instead of thinking, "I'm a failure," try thinking, "I made a mistake, but I can learn from it. What must I change to get this right the next time?" This is practicing self-compassion. Treat yourself with the same kindness and understanding you would offer a friend or relative.

You must also practice self-care. This includes things like going for a walk or listening to music. You can also use positive affirmations, such as "I am worthy and deserving of love and respect," to enhance feelings of positive self-worth. Say your affirmation either out loud or in your mind. I recommend doing this at least ten times in the morning and ten times before bed. You may not believe your affirmation at first, but over time, you usually realize that your affirmation is true. You are worthy and deserving of love and respect—no question about it.

Focusing on your strengths and accomplishments is helpful to lessen self-judgment. We tend to focus on our weaknesses and flaws when overly critical of ourselves. Make a list of your achievements, big or small, and remind yourself of them when you start to doubt yourself.

Always seek support from others. Talking to a friend, family member, or therapist can help you question your perspective and feel less alone. In addition, it's essential to surround yourself with those who love and support you - the people in what I call your "inner circle." Reflect on those who love and support you to fight off negative core beliefs formed in the past. Recognize that you are cared for and loved as you are. This can move you toward a greater sense of self-worth and increase your confidence.

Self-acceptance is the key to lowering the intensity of self-judgment. Accepting yourself and being compassionate toward yourself will help resolve negative self-reflection and judgment. You are who you are, and accepting who you are, both the good and the bad, is essential.

Reflections

_____

_____

_____

_____

_____

_____

_____

_____

_____

_____

_____

_____

_____

_____

_____

_____

_____

_____

_____

_____

What changes do you want to make?

_____

_____

_____

_____

_____

_____

_____

What steps do you need to take to bring about change?

_____

_____

_____

_____

_____

_____

_____

_____

_____

_____

"I can be changed by what happens to me. But I refuse to be reduced by it."

— Maya Angelou

"You best teach others about healthy boundaries by enforcing yours."

— Bryant McGill

14. USING THE PROTECTIVE BOUNDARY

Victimhood

Most of us have been unfairly criticized by another person. When this happens, we can be overcome by feelings of powerlessness. We believe nothing we can do or say will stop the unhappy or angry person from criticizing us.

We may think that people, even our loved ones, say mean and hurtful things to us because there is something wrong with us. Somehow, things are our fault. You may think, "This is just a mean, nasty person. They are just a hater!"

All too often, hurt pride and feelings of powerlessness make you falsely believe you are destined to be victimized and hurt repeatedly. You mistake the mean words of others as facts about yourself. You internalize them and judge yourself as a result. But you think, "This mean person is someone to hate, and I won't stand for it anymore." The question to ask is: why do you and what can you do?

The Role of Resentment – A Self-Inflicting Wound

As a result of being hurt by another person, you may feel resentment. You resent how you've been treated and the disrespect they treated you with. But, you say nothing and swallow your resentments whole. When you do this, you are trapping this negative energy in your body, and it slowly eats away at you. Why do you let the hatred and intolerance of others inside? It just doesn't make sense.

Those with healthy self-esteem accept themselves for who they are. They believe, at a core level, that they are valuable people.

When you are verbally attacked, remember that taking this inside of you is illogical. This means you must be self-protective and not let the mean words of others injure you. The hatred and mean-spirited nature of others don't *belong to you*. They originated outside of yourself, so it makes no sense for you to let them in and become a part of you.

You may carry resentful anger because of what the person has said or done. At the very least, harboring resentments is a waste of valuable energy. I always say that we have 100% of energy each day. How much of it do you want to spend on resenting another person? How much happiness are you denying yourself by being angry and resentful toward those who wronged you?

You may find yourself lingering in "victimhood." You can't change things, and you blame others for hurting you. This is why learning to protect yourself with boundaries is so important. Holding a resentment is like drinking poison and waiting for the other person to die. To not be a victim, you need to set protective boundaries.

What is a Protective Boundary?

To help you not take in the negativity that comes your way - judgment, disrespect, and anger - I tell people to practice doing this: Imagine yourself wearing a wet suit. You are covered by it head to toe. Recognize the wet suit as part of yourself. Then, when negativity comes at you, imagine the words hitting your wet suit, and see the words roll down the wet suit and hit the floor. You will likely feel the initial jab of the words, but if you imagine the words rolling off your wet suit and hitting the floor, you will not take them in, and you will have successfully implemented your protective boundary.

To let in the positive - love, caring, and support - imagine a little door inside the wet suit that is up by your face, with a handle on the inside that only you can open. Pull the door open to let in the positive. When practicing this exercise, be careful not to wall yourself off from the world. The wet suit is only there to protect you, not to cut you off from the world around you. I teach this psychological exercise to my clients, and I am told it works. I use this technique myself, and it has become an essential part of living a happier life.

Self-Worth

We are often taught that mean people don't like themselves, and they unload their negative feelings on others. However, when we look at the evidence, it becomes clear that nasty people choose offending behaviors. They mistreat others through word and deed because they lack a healthy sense of self-worth. They may also prey on those who also struggle with low self-worth. They do this to feel powerful and good about who they are. This is called being *"greater than."* This person acts better than everyone and uses negativity to put others down.

Being "Greater Than" And "Less Than"

Those of us who get hurt by the words or deeds of others think of ourselves as *"less than."* Feeling less than is when you feel like you are less than other people, that you are below them because you don't measure up. You don't fit in, and you can do nothing right. You are a failure.

People with a healthy sense of self-worth don't think they are "greater than" or "less than." Instead, they accept who they are. To stay true to their positive sense of self-worth, they don't need to act "greater than" or "less than" others to feel good about themselves. They already feel good about themselves.

Individuals with a healthy sense of self-worth protect themselves from abuse by setting appropriate boundaries. They stand up for themselves by speaking up. This is using the external boundary. They aren't affected by people who attack them because they have an appropriate level of self-worth that protects them from verbal abuse. If you have a solid sense of self-worth, what others say or do is of no consequence. It does not affect you because you feel good about who you are.

Those with a healthy sense of self-worth accept themselves for who they are. They believe, at a core level, that they are valuable people. They understand that everyone makes mistakes and that mistakes don't define who they are. Unlike individuals with low self-worth, they accept their mistakes and view them as opportunities to learn and grow. You can work to create this yourself. I suggest using an affirmation like "I am not a failure because I make mistakes. I just make mistakes."

You can learn to set protective boundaries through mindfulness and practice. Boundaries are an incredible thing. Setting boundaries allows you to put an end to feeling victimized and gives you the ability to choose your own path. Boundary setting is empowering and can change your life.

When you set boundaries, you increase your confidence and sense of self-worth because you are telling yourself that *you are worth protecting*. When you fail to set boundaries, you tell yourself you aren't worth protecting. If you believe you aren't worth protecting, your self-worth will suffer. By protecting yourself, you have acted kindly toward yourself. Taking care of yourself inherently leads to increased feelings of self-worth. When you set the protective boundary, you realize that you are worthy of protection from abuse, which means one thing: you are a person of value. This, of course, has always been true.

Reflections

What changes do you want to make?

_____

_____

_____

_____

_____

_____

What steps do you need to take to bring about change?

_____

_____

_____

_____

_____

_____

_____

_____

_____

"The anxiety of worry is almost always worse than the actual consequences. Stop worrying and start doing."

— James Clear

15. UNDERSTANDING WORRY

Breaking the Cycle

Breaking the worry cycle is one of the most challenging tasks some of us undertake. We worry about big things, like losing our job, or small things, like cleaning the house. Sometimes all we can see is the worst-case scenario. We feel trapped by anxiety and find it near impossible to enjoy life.

I always tell clients that we are given a finite amount of energy each day. Of the energy you have each day, I suspect you don't want to expend any of it on worry and anxiety. The time you spend worrying is a waste of your daily energy. Remember that anxiety and worry do not predict what happens in your everyday life.

We all worry. But, worry that is unstoppable, recurrent, highly intense, and unproductive is often related to 'generalized anxiety disorder.' Generalized anxiety disorder can be distilled down to this: you live with fear and anxiety almost daily.

Worry, at its core, is an emotional response to threat and uncertainty. It is a cognitive process often involving repetitive thoughts about negative outcomes or worst-case scenarios. You can begin to address worry by recognizing it as normal in response to your daily problems.

Worrying tremendously impacts your mental, emotional, and physical well-being. It can lead to increased stress, health problems, and sleep problems. Worry brings suffering, as those who worry incessantly often live in a state of high anxiety.

What Leads to Consistent and Intense Worry?

Consider these factors:

Catastrophizing

Thinking and focusing only on negative or catastrophic future events.

High Anxiety

This anxiety sometimes leads to physical problems (upset stomach, restlessness, muscle tightness, and heart problems). High anxiety can be described as an extreme nervous sensation. However, unlike having a panic attack, high anxiety can sometimes feel like it gets worse and worse.

Inability to Tolerate Life's Uncertainty

This often leads to perfectionistic and controlling behaviors. Those who can't tolerate uncertainty do all they can to control their outside environment and try to stop any imagined catastrophic event from happening.

Failure to Imagine Outcomes

No matter how often we think about avoiding negative outcomes in life experiences, we fail to think of adequate solutions to imagined problems.

Dysfunctional Beliefs

Usually adapted from past negative life experiences, we begin to believe - then become certain - that the worst will always happen.

One of the most effective ways to combat worry is by questioning our thoughts and the emotions that are related to those thoughts. Often, worry stems from irrational, dysfunctional thoughts about the future. To combat worry, you must challenge and reframe these thoughts. Only then can your level of worry be reduced or resolved.

Acceptance and Completing a Life Inventory

The concept of acceptance is the key to fighting off high anxiety and lowering the intensity of worry. You must learn to accept yourself and your life as it is. Acceptance is a way of living. How good are you at accepting yourself and your life? Do you accept reality as it is? If you accept reality as it is, you are free to act in ways that bring greater peace and serenity to your life. Acceptance requires building a new perspective on your life and its outcomes.

To help you learn to accept your life as it is, it is helpful to take an inventory of past experiences and their outcomes. What happened over your lifetime? Were all outcomes catastrophic? Most of us can recall some negative (even disastrous) outcomes, while other experiences were within normal limits. An accurate look at life's experiences and outcomes can teach you that life is filled with good and bad. This makes it clear that worrying wastes our energy as we cannot know which direction life will take us.

The concept of acceptance is the key to changing your life and lowering worry. We must learn to accept ourselves and our lives as they are.

Coping With Worry

When you worry, consider these strategies to provide you with a sense of control and relief: do deep breathing exercises, start journaling, engage in physical activity, do yoga, seek the support of friends and family, and practice relaxation techniques like meditation or progressive muscle relaxation. These are all tools to help you worry less.

Challenging your negative core beliefs can also help lessen worry and anxiety. For example, when you are caught up in a worry spiral, authors David Clark and Aaron Beck suggest you ask yourself these three questions:

1) What is the worst thing that can happen?

2) What is the best thing that can happen?

And,

3) What is most likely going to happen?

If you ask yourself these three questions, you will likely discover that most of the time, 'What is most likely going to happen' is the answer.

Worrying wastes your daily energy and does not help you find the solutions you seek. Of 100% of your daily energy, how much of it do you want to spend worrying? The answer, of course, is none.

Reflections

_____
_____
_____
_____
_____
_____
_____
_____
_____
_____
_____
_____
_____
_____
_____
_____
_____
_____
_____
_____

What changes do you want to make?

_____

_____

_____

_____

_____

_____

_____

What steps do you need to take to bring about change?

_____

_____

_____

_____

_____

_____

_____

_____

_____

_____

"The secret of getting ahead is getting started. The secret to getting started is breaking your overwhelming tasks into small manageable tasks, and then starting on the first one."

— *Mark Twain*

16. BEFORE THERAPY BEGINS

The Importance of Self-Care

Before therapy begins, I always ask my clients about self-care - are you taking care of yourself physically and practicing basic self-care?

Mental health problems like depression and anxiety cannot be successfully treated if an underlying physical condition needs attention. So, when was the last time you visited your primary care doctor for a check-up? And if you don't have a primary care doctor, I suggest you find one now.

Get a Physical

I always recommend getting a physical examination before beginning therapy. Working in therapy to reduce and resolve mental health symptoms may be ineffective if you have a physical problem that affects your mood. You don't want to spend weeks in treatment and then discover you have a hormonal imbalance creating feelings of depression and anxiety. Before you start psychotherapy, it is imperative that you visit your doctor for a checkup. This is an essential part of self-care.

Mental health problems like depression and anxiety cannot be successfully treated if an underlying physical condition needs attention.

Before therapy, you must also inventory any medications or supplements you take. Some medications can affect your mood. Review your medications with your primary care doctor or psychiatrist and tell them if you are having any mental health symptoms. I suggest you write down all signs and symptoms of physical and psychological problems. Bringing in a list helps the doctor understand in detail why you came to see them and helps you remember all of the issues you need to report.

If you are taking psychotropic medications to treat mental health problems such as anxiety or depression and you don't think they are working (or not working well enough), be sure to report all of the emotional problems you are having and the intensity of those problems. Then, be proactive and ask your doctor if you need a medication change.

What Do You Ingest?

During your initial assessment, I review everything you put into your body with you. I want to know what foods, drinks, supplements, and medications you ingest. Many mental health problems can be caused by simple things that are overlooked.

For example, if you come in with symptoms of anxiety and then tell me that you drink sodas, energy drinks, or coffee each day, you will realize that all of these drinks contain caffeine, and too much caffeine can cause anxiety. If you cut down or stop drinking caffeinated beverages, it is easy to re-assess your level of anxiety.

Nicotine can also lead to anxiety. Are you a smoker or vapor, or do you use nicotine gum or lozenges? You need to inventory how much nicotine you ingest. Although it is difficult to stop nicotine use, stopping altogether or knowing how much you consume is essential.

Alcohol and drug use are a crucial part of your inventory. Alcohol can cause depression, marijuana can cause hallucinations, and cocaine can create extreme anxiety. If you are an active alcoholic or addict, you may be experiencing symptoms of many different mental health disorders. Take an inventory to determine if your substance use may be causing psychological symptoms. If your symptoms disappear when you are not using substances, you may be experiencing substance-induced symptoms.

Make Needed Changes

Exercising is another form of self-care. You may dread it, or it may be low on your priority list, but regular exercise has physical and mental health benefits. Exercising can be an essential act of self-care. It helps you maintain good physical health and mental health.

Staying social is also an act of self-care. Are you isolating, or are you spending time with others? Nothing feeds depression more than isolation. Getting out and visiting friends and relatives or inviting them over for a visit is another act of self-care. If you are depressed, you may not have the energy to get out. If so, start calling your inner circle people - those who love and support you and that you love and support in return.

Alcohol can cause depression, marijuana can cause hallucinations, and cocaine can create extreme anxiety. If you are an active alcoholic or addict, you may be experiencing symptoms of many different mental health disorders. Your substance use may be causing psychological symptoms.

There may be small things in your life that may be impacting your mood that you can eliminate without much effort. For example, sit down and pay some bills to lower anxiety, go through and organize a pile of mail, or clean your home (at least 1 room to start).

What to Expect

Psychotherapy is an emotional process, so you must acknowledge and prepare for the emotions that may arise while you are in therapy. Therapy involves exploring difficult emotions relating to your history and present life. For therapy to be successful, it is crucial that you be open, honest, and willing to engage with your therapist.

Therapy is not a quick fix or a magical solution. It requires time, effort, and commitment. Understand that progress may take time, and there may be ups and downs along the way. Having realistic expectations can help you stay motivated and committed to your therapy.

Most people never go to therapy, not because they wouldn't benefit from it, but because they aren't committed to working on themselves in an intense and focused way. Working with a therapist can be life-changing, and I, of course, highly recommend it.

Reflections

What changes do you want to make?

_____

_____

_____

_____

_____

_____

_____

What steps do you need to take to bring about change?

_____

_____

_____

_____

_____

_____

_____

_____

_____

_____

135

"I set boundaries not to offend you but to respect myself."

— Unknown

17. SETTING FAMILY BOUNDARIES

Its Challenges and Solutions

No one seems to traverse our boundaries like family members. Although you are an adult, parents can sometimes (or all the time) treat you like the child you once were. Frustration (anger) and embarrassment (shame) may be the emotions you feel when it happens.

Has this happened to you, or am I the only one? Your mom starts telling stories of how difficult you were as a child (in front of other people), and you find yourself stunned, so much so that you say nothing in your defense. Or, perhaps your father tells you that you spend too much money - even though you have a good job and don't have money problems. These examples can make you so angry that you may never want to speak to them again! Family members tell you what to do, what is right and wrong, and what needs to be changed in your life. Do you say anything? Perhaps now is the time to learn how to set family boundaries.

Unlike setting boundaries with people who are not family members, setting boundaries with family can be more difficult. They may disrespect your boundary setting and push back hard.

Your family members usually want you to stay the same as you've always been. A family is a system. Therefore, if you change, the system must change, and your family members must change. They may try to keep you how you've always been because *they don't want to change.* Your family members can push and push and disrespect your boundaries in the process. Parents tend to want the family system to remain static; they may even want you to be how they remember you as a child - forever.

If you don't work protective boundaries, you are telling yourself that you are unworthy of protecting. If you are not worth protecting, your sense of self-worth diminishes.

If you don't work any boundaries, you are wide open to all of the negativity that comes your way. Being 'wide open' means ingesting and letting in all the negative things people say or do. Your life can be painful and chaotic when you don't have boundaries. The meanness and criticism of others hit you straight on. Putting what are called 'protective boundaries' in place can protect you from taking in all of the negativity coming at you.

Protective Boundaries

To set protective boundaries, I instruct my clients to wear a 'wet suit.' I have outlined this in an earlier chapter, but I believe it is worth describing again. Wearing a wet suit is a visualization exercise in which you image yourself covered in a wet suit from head to toe. The wet suit completely protects you, and the only way in is through a small door up by your face. The door has a handle only on the inside, allowing you to decide when to open it and what to let in. To be protective, I tell people to imagine

138

seeing the words of negative comments hit the wet suit, roll off of it, and fall to the floor. You may feel the initial jab of the words when they come, but the wet suit gives you protection and the ability to avoid taking negative and hurtful things inside. When positives like love and connection come, you can open your small door from the inside and let it in. This allows you to let in the positive while keeping you protected from the negative.

The negative may sting, but when you practice protecting yourself and visualizing the negative words rolling off the wet suit, the negative dissipates. Working the protective boundary requires mindfulness and an awareness of what is happening from moment to moment. If you wear the wet suit, you are no longer open to being hurt so easily. You are now working the protective boundary.

Family Time

But, family members may try to break through your boundaries consistently. They know you haven't worked protective boundaries in the past, so they know how to 'get to you.' When someone tries to traverse your protective boundary repeatedly and discovers they *can* get inside, they may exploit this vulnerability. They will try it repeatedly once they learn they can successfully surpass your boundary. You must always be consistent and self-protective, especially with family. They will see no reason to stop pushing if they can break past your boundary even once.

When it comes to our families, being protective may seem impossible. Remember, your family wants you to be as vulnerable as you've always been to keep the family system unchanged. They may push and push and push to keep the system unchanged - but you must be vigilant and set your protective boundary over and over again. Instead of instantly reacting to something negative they've said to you, pause for a moment and imagine seeing the words roll off.

Setting External Boundaries

Setting external boundaries is when you actually say something to those who do not respect your boundaries. Author Pia Mellody explains that one effective way to set an external boundary is to say:

"When you _____, I feel _____, and I would prefer _____."

"Mom, when you tell me to cut my hair, I feel hurt, and I would prefer that you stop doing it!" Taking responsibility for your feelings lowers the defensiveness of the person you are speaking to. Setting this boundary may or may not work as the offender may or may not change their behaviors. Regardless, you have said what you needed to, spoken your truth, and acted in a self-protective way.

Setting an external boundary with family can seem ineffective, as they may ignore ANY boundary you set. But, as mentioned, you may need to set your boundaries over and over with family members. Family members will also try to traverse your boundaries because they know you'll tolerate their bad behavior. They behave differently with friends because they know they won't tolerate these behaviors.

To effectively set external boundaries with family members, take time to identify your needs so that you can set clear and specific boundaries. Determine what behaviors, actions, or topics of conversation are acceptable and unacceptable. To clarify your boundaries, it can be helpful to write them down.

When discussing boundaries with your family, it's important to communicate assertively yet respectfully. Think through who you are going to talk to and when. Use "I" statements when you express how certain behaviors affect you and explain why you must set boundaries.

I believe setting personal boundaries protects not just who you are today but also your "inner child." Would you allow a child to be treated the way you are being treated? Of course not. Be true to yourself and the child within by being self-protective. When you do, you are telling yourself you are worth protecting, and as a result, your sense of self-worth increases. If you don't work protective boundaries, you are telling yourself that you are unworthy of protection. If you are not worth protecting, your sense of self-worth diminishes. You will discover that you cannot build self-worth without being self-protective and working protective boundaries.

When setting boundaries with family, remember that they often push hard to get past them because they want the family system to remain unchanged. Therefore, it is essential to be consistent in setting boundaries with your family. If you aren't, family members will have little reason to stop their negative behaviors.

Reflections

_____

_____

_____

_____

_____

_____

_____

_____

_____

_____

_____

_____

_____

_____

_____

_____

_____

_____

_____

_____

_____

What changes do you want to make?

_____

_____

_____

_____

_____

_____

_____

What steps do you need to take to bring about change?

_____

_____

_____

_____

_____

_____

_____

_____

_____

"You must do things you think you cannot do."

— *Eleanor Roosevelt*

18. WHAT IS LIFE COACHING?

A Brief Comparison of Life Coaching and Psychotherapy

Personal and professional coaching is now the most sought-after way for individuals who seek help motivating and moving forward toward reaching their goals. I am often asked which is better – life coaching or therapy. The two seem similar but are different, as I briefly outline below.

Therapy or Life Coaching?

Psychotherapy is a method of treating mental health disorders such as depression and anxiety. Psychotherapy focuses on resolving or reducing the symptoms of mental health disorders. Clients describe their symptoms, and the therapist uses their knowledge of psychological treatments and clinical experience to help.

The client and therapist discuss the client's history and current life to determine how these may negatively impact the client's life. The therapist then listens and provides feedback to assist the client in changing their perspective on the past and addressing problems they are experiencing in their current life.

145

They discuss new ways of viewing themselves, their history, and their everyday life. Behavior change and symptom reduction can result as the client changes their way of thinking and seeing themselves, others, and the world. Cognitive therapy asserts that thoughts lead to feelings, and feelings lead to behavior. Therefore, change your thoughts, and your behavior will change as well. Good therapists do not give advice. Instead, they assist clients in seeing and understanding their lives more clearly. The goal is to help the client build insight into their problems so they can change dysfunctional thinking and behavior. Psychotherapy is extremely powerful and life-changing.

Coaching is a Partnership

Personal and professional coaching is a partnership. There is an inherent power differential in psychotherapy, as the client looks to the therapist to help them resolve symptoms. This is called the medical model, where one party is the patient, and the other is the doctor. Individuals who come for life coaching are not seeking relief from psychiatric symptoms. Instead, life coaching clients seek inspiration, increased motivation, and assistance in achieving their life goals.

In life coaching, clients specify the goals they are trying to reach and begin identifying what is blocking them from reaching their goals. Then together, the client and coach work to resolve and remove what is blocking the client from reaching their goals through planning and execution. Coaches are teachers, sounding boards, motivators, and planners.

Many clients will work in psychotherapy while also working in life coaching. Sometimes clients discover that one of the blocks preventing them from reaching their goals requires therapy. For example, having depression will severely impact your ability to motivate yourself toward goal attainment. Therefore, to move forward in life coaching, clients will work in therapy to resolve or reduce the impact of their depression.

The coach's job is to help you clarify and uncover what is most important to you, assist you in identifying the goals you want to attain, and work with you on overcoming what is blocking you from meeting your goals.

The Coach's Job

The coach's job is to help you clarify and uncover what is most important to you, assist you in identifying the goals you want to attain, and work with you on overcoming what is blocking you from meeting your goals. A coach works with you to create plans that lead to goal attainment and helps you identify and change counter-productive behaviors that may be blocking your success. Coaching is for people seeking greater success in meeting personal and professional goals. Life coaching, like therapy, is very powerful and is a life-changing experience.

I have been a psychotherapist for 30 years and witnessed miraculous changes in those I have worked with. In life coaching, I have seen people dramatically change, overcome what is blocking them from meeting their goals, and find the success they seek.

Reflections

_____

_____

_____

_____

_____

_____

_____

_____

_____

_____

_____

_____

_____

_____

_____

_____

_____

_____

_____

What changes do you want to make?

_____

_____

_____

_____

_____

_____

_____

What steps do you need to take to bring about change?

_____

_____

_____

_____

_____

_____

_____

_____

_____

"It is the client who knows what hurts, what directions to go, what problems are crucial, what experiences have been deeply buried."

— Carl Rogers

19. PERSON-CENTERED THERAPY

Why I Use It

Therapist, teacher, and researcher Carl Rogers introduced what is now known as person-centered psychotherapy in the late 1950s. This therapeutic method shifts therapy away from the therapist's role as "the expert" to focus on how the therapist and client can work together on problems and solutions. Much of how psychotherapy is practiced today uses parts of this method.

When new clients ask about my therapeutic methods, I explain that I provide psychodynamic psychotherapy and cognitive therapy within a Rogerian person-centered framework. In this person-centered framework, I strive to support personal growth by providing a non-judgmental therapy experience and what is known as unconditional positive regard. Rogers posits that personal growth occurs when the therapist provides unconditional positive regard and a safe, non-judgmental environment for clients to work in.

Personal growth can only occur when there is a connected relationship between you and your therapist.

To Provide Rogerian Person-Centered Psychotherapy, the Following Conditions Must Exist

- Personal growth can only occur when there is a strong bond between you and your therapist. Here, Rogers stresses the need for a robust, connected relationship. He states that for you to experience personal growth, you and your therapist must have a connected relationship.

- Anxiety and fear result from an 'incongruence' between self-image and daily experiences. You may be unaware of the clouded way you see reality as the result of your inner core beliefs. You and the therapist work together to identify these beliefs and how they impact your life and view of the world.

- Your therapist must be genuine. For your personal growth to occur, the therapist must be true and understand themselves when they work with you. This means that the therapist needs to be self-aware if they are to understand you and your experiences.

- The therapist must provide unconditional positive regard when working with you. This is the foundation upon which the therapeutic relationship rests. Providing unconditional positive regard means that the therapist accepts all of you and who you are, free of judgment.

- The therapist must be empathic. Empathy is the ability to understand and relate to your experiences and emotions. Your therapist's ability to relate to what you bring to the relationship is critical to your personal growth.

- By providing unconditional positive regard and a non-judgmental environment in therapy, you can be who you are. You can only change and grow in therapy if you feel safe sharing all of who you are.

You must feel safe and understood when participating in psychotherapy. When a therapist uses Rogerian person-centered methods, you gain a true understanding of who you are, which allows you to grow and change.

Reflections

_____

_____

_____

_____

_____

_____

_____

_____

_____

_____

_____

_____

_____

_____

_____

_____

_____

_____

_____

_____

_____

What changes do you want to make?

_____

_____

_____

_____

_____

_____

_____

What steps do you need to take to bring about change?

_____

_____

_____

_____

_____

_____

_____

_____

_____

PART TWO: OUR RELATIONSHIPS

"A successful marriage requires falling in love many times, always with the same person."

— Mignon McLaughlin

20. MARRIAGE COUNSELING

Examining Your Relationship Rules

Why do we disagree and argue so much? When a couple comes in for marriage or relationship counseling, I often discover that disagreements and arguments stem from the different ways they learned about what a relationship is. Your rule book for how a relationship should be is what you learned growing up. Watching your parents or caregivers relate to one another is the way things are supposed to be, right? Why would you expect your relationship to be any different? You argue because you and your partner see how things "should be" in different ways. When a couple disagrees, they attempt to convince each other that their way is the best way.

There are many books on marriage and relationships, but there isn't one instruction manual that is required reading. Therefore, when you get married, you must blend what you learned about how relationships work with how your partner learned about how relationships work. Sometimes what you think and what your partner thinks is vastly different. And this can lead to a lot of arguments and disagreements.

What was the 'rule book' your parents or caregivers had? For example, were your parents kind, attentive, and supportive of each other? Or were they bossy, anxious, or angry? Did they support each other in most things, or did you hear screaming matches and disagreements? Did your parents have a relationship of equals, or was one of your parents in charge? And who did you learn from? Mom, Dad, grandparents, or others?

Marriage and relationship problems begin when what I call 'integration failure' occurs. This is when you and your partner overlay your understanding of how a relationship should be (learned in childhood) onto your current relationship, and you fail to integrate them successfully.

What you learned about relationships as a child affects your marriage or relationship in ways you probably don't want to admit. "How could I make the same mistakes they did?" I suspect you applied what you learned about what not to do, but there may be areas that you overlooked. Examine your behavior to identify the different ways you and your partner have of doing things. This not only applies to your relationship but your everyday life as well.

The Rules of Marriage and Relationships

Recognizing the rules you bring to your relationship is essential to fixing it. You come to your relationship with a unique view of how relationships 'should be' - as does your partner. Your understanding of how a relationship should be can include the following:

- what your family values are,

- what your beliefs are regarding how your partner should behave,

- what role each partner is expected to fulfill,

- and, what your expectations of your partner are.

Integration Failure

Marriage and relationship problems begin when what I call 'integration failure' occurs. This is when you and your partner overlay your understanding of how a relationship should be (learned in childhood) onto your current relationship, and you fail to integrate them successfully.

This is where problems are most often found. This keeps couples stuck. Integration failure is found in your arguments and disagreements. When you look at them closely, the evidence is usually there. Integration failure is what I see when a couple comes to me for marriage counseling or couples therapy.

Uncovering what you learned about relationships from your parents and caregivers must be addressed in your marital therapy or couples counseling from the beginning. Successfully integrating your beliefs about how a relationship should be a primary goal. This is when you can begin negotiating around these beliefs and write your own rule book on how to have a successful relationship.

While I work with couples sorting out their rule book, I begin addressing the state of their friendship. Most people believe poor communication is at the heart of a bad relationship. Communication is usually a big part of the problem, but the first thing to address is the state of your friendship. Do you even like each other? Being friends is the foundation upon which your relationship rebuilds. If you don't even like your partner, it is time to find out why and work on fixing it. Learn to be friends again. One simple way to begin is to talk about why you decided to commit to each other in the first place.

It is challenging to fix your broken connection on your own, especially when you consider the stressors of everyday life - be it children, jobs, money, your parents, or your in-law's needs. A marriage counselor or couples therapist provides a forum to work exclusively on the relationship and what it needs. Counseling helps you find common ground to improve the relationship and create a stronger connection.

The best thing you have going for you is that you are an adult, and adults can choose how to behave.

Address Issues Reasonably

How issues and disagreements are handled is another critical consideration within your marriage or relationship. It is difficult to find solutions when tempers flare. Marriage counseling provides an environment where you can reasonably address problems and disagreements. This neutral setting allows you to see things rationally, which is the key to resolving conflicts. I start with household negotiations, "If you take out the trash, I will make the bed." Starting negotiations around household responsibilities, simple as it seems, can make a huge difference. If you agree to do something and stick to your word, there is nothing to argue about. I always point out that the best thing you have going for you is that you are an adult, and *adults can choose how to behave.*

A marriage counselor will also provide an outsider's perspective on your relationship and its problems. You may get wrapped up in your own way of thinking and seeing, and having a third party provide a professional view of the problems is essential.

Examine Your Communication Style

How you communicate is just as important as the words you say. What tone do you use when you communicate? Do you speak loudly? Negative tones and inflection can render a good point moot and lead to heated arguments. A marriage counselor will offer new methods of communication that focus on mutual understanding and respect.

When you begin marriage counseling, each of you must be honest in discussing why you believe you need counseling in the first place. But it is crucial to discuss what you both learned about what a committed relationship should be like and what you bring to your current relationship. What do you expect from your partner and why? Writing a rule book that you both agree on needs to be negotiated. Your therapist will help you better understand how your different views contribute to your problem. To succeed, you must be willing to hear each other and work together to rekindle the friendship you valued so much in the past.

Reflections

What changes do you want to make?

_____

_____

_____

_____

_____

_____

_____

What steps do you need to take to bring about change?

_____

_____

_____

_____

_____

_____

_____

_____

_____

_____

"Marriage is not just spiritual communion. It is also remembering to take out the trash."

— Dr. Joyce Brothers

21. COMMUNICATION IN MARRIAGE

A Quick Lesson

When I meet with some couples, I listen as they go back and forth about why everything is their partner's fault. If only they would change, the relationship would be fixed.

When this happens, I tell them to reflect on their own behaviors and clean up their side of the street. My meaning is simple. You must look at what you say and do that contributes to your relationship problems and change your behaviors. Relationships are dynamic, and each of you plays a role. If you reflect on your behaviors and begin working on what you must change - cleaning up your side of the street - your relationship will inevitably improve.

When you begin couples therapy, I recommend you reflect and take an inventory of why you behave as you do in relationships. As difficult, unpleasant, or painful as it may be, reflect on 1) what you learned about relationships growing up and 2) your relationship history. As you reflect on the past, consider whether your parent's or caregiver's behaviors, how you behaved, or what happened in past relationships impact your relationship today.

Improving Communication

A simple way to improve your communication is to learn to listen better. This requires you to practice what is called active listening. Active listening is when you pay close attention to your partner's words, repeat what they said back to them to verify that you understood them, and ask questions if you need clarification. Second, if you aren't showing your partner empathy, you should start. This is when you understand your partner's perspective, put yourself in their shoes, and acknowledge their feelings. Also, work to validate your partner's feelings by acknowledging that you heard and understood what they are saying. Finally, always take responsibility for your behaviors when you know you are wrong.

After seeing progress in your listening skills, I recommend this exercise: Sit across from each other and decide who will go first. Then, one of you is allowed to talk uninterrupted for 10 minutes. While you talk, your partner must concentrate and listen only. They aren't allowed to defend themselves or explain away anything. They must sit and give you 10 minutes of uninterrupted time to be heard. When your partner is done speaking, you now have 10 minutes of uninterrupted time. When it's your turn to talk, focus on yourself. If your partner shared first, do not defend yourself when it is your turn. Use "I" statements when speaking to keep defensiveness low. Having this time to open up safely, without being attacked, lets you express your thoughts, emotions, and needs freely. This quick and simple exercise is a vital step in communicating clearly with each other.

You can also improve communication by *making time* to communicate. With busy schedules and other commitments, making time for meaningful conversations can be difficult. However, setting aside a specific time each day or week to communicate and connect can help build intimacy and strengthen your relationship. This time could be as simple as sitting down to have dinner together.

Take responsibility for cleaning up 'your side of the street.' This means you must look at what you say or do that contributes to the problem and change your words and behaviors.

Communication Styles

You need to be aware of the different communication styles that you may each have. For example, you may prefer direct communication, or you may prefer a softer approach. Understanding these differences and being willing to change can help prevent misunderstandings and miscommunications. Patience and willingness to adapt to each other's communication style is essential.

Improving communication in your marriage is crucial for building intimacy, understanding, and respect between you. You should create a safe and non-judgmental space for open communication, practice listening skills, make time for communication, understand each other's communication styles, and seek outside help when necessary. By implementing these strategies, you can enhance your communication, strengthen your relationship, and rebuild a foundation for growth and greater happiness.

Reflections

_____

_____

_____

_____

_____

_____

_____

_____

_____

_____

_____

_____

_____

_____

_____

_____

_____

_____

_____

_____

_____

_____

_____

_____

What changes do you want to make?

_____

_____

_____

_____

_____

_____

_____

_____

What steps do you need to take to bring about change?

_____

_____

_____

_____

_____

_____

_____

_____

_____

_____

_____

"I'm not upset that you lied to me, I'm upset that from now on I can't believe you."

— *Friedrich Nietzsche*

22. SNOOPING

Distrust and Its Destructive Power

Most of us have our eyes focused on and our noses buried in our smartphones throughout the day. If we aren't browsing, we are texting or calling others. Today's communication technology is revolutionary, allowing us to call, text, and e-mail anyone quickly and easily.

Here's a question: have your communication skills improved as a result? You might conclude that all this furious communication would inevitably lead to better communication between people. But unfortunately, in my experience, this question does not have a straightforward answer.

The Dark Side

When I work with couples, I hear about the darker side of texting and e-mailing. Its mere existence can cause conflict and lead to distrust within committed relationships. Sometimes problems arise because of how often the two of you communicate. Do you call your partner multiple times a day?

Do you text 'Good morning?' What happens if you forget to text one morning?

Problems erupt when one partner discovers that the other has been texting or e-mailing someone else - someone who isn't them - and someone they perceive as a threat to the relationship.

Most people snoop because of one or two things. One is, "I'm afraid of losing him." The second is, "I don't trust him." Driven by fear and anxiety, snoopers snoop, hoping to waylay their fears or confirm their suspicions.

If any of this sounds familiar, read on:

"I checked his phone and found text messages from an old girlfriend. Why didn't you tell me she had been texting you? How long has this been going on? Have you texted her back? When did this start? How can I trust you if I don't know who you're texting?"

or

"Her e-mail account was open on the tablet. I quickly looked, but then I couldn't help but snoop around. I couldn't believe what I found. She's been hiding e-mails from her ex-husband. Why would she keep old e-mails from her ex-husband? I'm her husband now, and she needs to cut ties with him. How can I trust her if I don't know who she's e-mailing? Who else has been contacting you?"

or

"I checked his phone and found dozens of text messages from a woman named Nancy. Who's Nancy? He told me she was just a friend from work, but they text each other over a dozen times each day. Some suggestive comments are going back and forth – what is all of this? Are you having an affair?"

or

"I was on the laptop and checked his browser history. You would not believe what he's been looking at."

or

"I was on the laptop and checked his browser history. There was no browser history - it had been erased. What is he doing that he's hiding from me?"

When I work with couples, one or both partners may confess to phone snooping, e-mail checking, and rapid-fire texting during fights ("I'm trying to work, and he continues texting me non-stop. It's compulsive and out of control. I can't go on like this.")

How Can I Trust You?

Why do people snoop? Most people snoop because of one or two things. One is, "I'm afraid of losing him." The second is, "I don't trust him." Driven by fear and anxiety, snoopers snoop, hoping to waylay their fears or confirm their suspicions.

But snooping can be dangerous. Upon discovering *possible* incriminating evidence, strong emotions can overpower the snooper and cloud their view of reality. Although there isn't enough evidence, a snooper's fear can lead them to jump to conclusions. Therefore, paying attention to the evidence in front of you is essential - what is real, not what might be real.

When you fail to do this, strong emotions can cloud your thinking and lead you to misinterpret and misunderstand what you find. For example, discovering that your partner recently received a text from an old boyfriend may be completely innocent.

When I work with couples, one or both partners may confess to phone snooping, e-mail checking, and rapid-fire texting during arguments.

The text came in, but she ignored it and did not respond. But when you discover it, fear kicks in and convinces you that a) she is going to leave me, b) she is starting an affair with or is having an affair with this man behind my back, or c) she has been communicating with this man for a long time and has been erasing all the texts between the two of them.

In these examples, snooping has made you feel unsafe, fearful, and distrustful. A misinterpretation of what you've uncovered can damage the intimacy and trust you and your partner share.

Before jumping to conclusions, consider what has shaken you. Examine the evidence. One text message does not prove any of the above. If you trust your partner, you will likely conclude that it's just an unsolicited text from a curious or lonely past partner. To avoid conflict, you and your partner can agree to keep each other informed of any incoming texts or e-mails that either of you receives from past partners.

Keeping your partner informed of unsolicited communication from an ex can help avoid misunderstandings and senseless arguments. Finding an old stash of e-mails your partner has saved written by her ex does not mean she is unhappy and coveting a past relationship. Instead, they may remind her of her youth, past life, and who she once was. They're just old e-mails, and your partner might simply be sentimental.

Trust is the very foundation upon which your relationship can grow. It creates a safe space where you and your partner can express yourself and be who you are. When you trust your partner, emotional security forms, allowing you to share your secret thoughts, dreams, and fears without fear of being judged

Why Trust is Essential

Trust is intimately linked to emotional intimacy—the deep sense of closeness, connection, and vulnerability between you and your partner. Trust must be established if emotional intimacy is to grow. It allows you to be who you really are - to be vulnerable and open with your partner. Doing this allows you both to feel accepted and loved unconditionally.

To be trustworthy, you must also honor your commitments. Relationships bring responsibilities, and to build trust in your relationship, you need to be reliable and someone your partner can turn to in a crisis.

Unfaithfulness

Sometimes your fears are realized, and you discover that your partner is having an affair - emotional or physical. You find yourself at a crossroads and must decide whether to leave the relationship or try to remain together.

Infidelity is one of the most devastating experiences in a relationship. The betrayal of trust can leave you feeling angry, hurt, and confused. If you decide to stay in the relationship, you may want to take some time to process your emotions. It is natural to feel emotions like anger, sadness, and confusion.

An open and honest conversation with your partner about what happened is vital. This conversation may be difficult, but it is essential for rebuilding trust and repairing the relationship. Ask your partner to be honest with you about what happened and why. Be prepared to listen to what they say, but tell your partner what you expect of them.

Deciding to Stay or Go

If you stay with your partner, establish clear boundaries and expectations for the relationship. You need to decide on what is acceptable and what is not acceptable behavior. It is crucial to be clear and direct in your communication and to hold your partner accountable for their actions. To rebuild, both partners must commit to sharing the whole truth. The unfaithful partner must come 100% clean, and if you have secrets to tell, now is the time for you to reveal them. Trust cannot re-establish itself until all secrets are revealed.

I always recommend working with a marriage counselor or a couples coach during this process. They will clarify the steps to rebuild your relationship and provide support and guidance while you move forward.

Staying with an unfaithful partner can create problems with texts, emails, and internet use. You may demand access to all three. However, the problem with monitoring your partner's communications is that it perpetuates your fear and never helps build trust between you. The continual checking sometimes takes on a life of its own. You end up monitoring your partner compulsively. If this occurs, your relationship is not moving forward, trust is not being rebuilt, and you live in fear.

Ultimately, it is up to you to decide what is best for you and your relationship. It may take time to rebuild trust and repair the damage caused by infidelity. Rebuilding and regaining trust is possible, but clear communication and a commitment to work through the issues must exist.

Reflections

What changes do you want to make?

_____

_____

_____

_____

_____

_____

_____

What steps do you need to take to bring about change?

_____

_____

_____

_____

_____

_____

_____

_____

_____

_____

"True love comes quietly, without banners or flashing lights. If you hear bells, get your ears checked."

— *Erich Segal*

23. GROWING A RELATIONSHIP

The Importance of Unconditional Acceptance

Fall in love. Idolize and worship your new partner. Think of them all the time - when you wake up and when you fall asleep. How fantastic relationships are in the beginning. It is important to cherish and remember this time. This is called the infatuation stage of your relationship. This is where you start, and it only comes once.

But, we all know that infatuation doesn't last. We are all on our best behavior during the first few months of a relationship. The reality, however, eventually begins to reveal itself. You learn more about your partner's attitudes toward the world, life, commitment, trust, and you. You begin to see your partner more clearly – the fog induced by infatuation begins to clear.

It is now time to take stock – to squint hard and see your partner as they truly are. Is this 'your person' or not? Can you envision a future with the person? Can you see spending your life together? Answering these questions is essential and part of the journey to finding the person you want to commit your life and heart to.

Unconditional Acceptance

Unconditional acceptance means that you accept your partner completely. It is an essential part of finding deeper emotional intimacy and happiness. If this is 'your person,' you must consider whether you can truly accept them for who they are, not who you want them to be. I have worked with many clients who made this mistake - expecting their partner to be someone else.

Unconditional acceptance means that you accept your partner fully. If this is really 'your person,' you must consider whether you can truly accept them for who they are, not who you want them to be.

Don't just look at the good stuff– the sex, the romantic texts, and the insightful exchange of gifts. I'm talking about everything. Of course, there are always characteristics your partner may have that you don't like - that may drive you up the wall - but if you are to grow love, you need to learn to accept and love your partner as they are.

But how? You discover piles of unhung clothes scattered all over her house. You find out she's a bit disorganized - well, no, she's really a slob. As the relationship becomes more serious, you must consider whether you can live the rest of your life accepting this. If you don't, your future together may be an unhappy one. Bringing her around to neatness and seeing how wonderful being organized is may be impossible.

Trying to change your partner leads to unhappiness. Don't have expectations of your partner that they cannot meet. Unhappiness lives in unmet expectations. To be truly happy, you must avoid trying to make your partner more and more like you. They are their own person, with their own peculiar way of doing things (as are you). This can be a challenge, but you must accept your partner unconditionally. Sometimes this means doing something with your partner that they enjoy, but you don't. However, being giving of yourself is crucial to building a loving relationship.

How Do I Trust?

You have willingly given your heart to your partner during the first few months. This is the way of new love. Soon, the question of trustworthiness must be examined.

"Can I trust this person? Will they love me and stand with me? Will they be careful not to hurt me?" These tend to be the questions you ask yourself as your relationship grows. Trusting a new partner can be a challenge, especially for people who have been hurt in past relationships. You must take time to find the answers to these questions.

"Should I trust?" and "How do I build trust?" are different questions. Once you have answered the first, you can start thinking about the second. So how do you build trust?

Before building trust, you must learn what trust means to you and your partner. This sounds obvious, but maybe not. For example, she might think being friends with old lovers is okay while you don't. You must discover if you share an understanding of what a trusting relationship is. Do you share its bounds, its rules, and its expectations? Answering these

185

questions is essential. Be specific to avoid future problems and misunderstandings. Are your expectations the same as hers? Communicate clearly when you set your boundaries and explain your behavioral expectations. Have open and honest discussions about this. You may not agree on all things, but people rarely do. If you disagree, take the time to understand your partner's view and try to negotiate an agreement that works for you both. Talking about what trust means helps to build trust and grow your relationship.

Ways to Build Trust in Your Relationship

Keep Your Promises

To demonstrate that you are trustworthy, keep the promises you make. Here I'm talking about both the big things and the small things. Don't forget that some of the small things may be the big things to your partner. When you're running late, call or text. Walk the dog as promised and do the dishes. Keep your promises, no matter how insignificant you may believe them to be. Being trustworthy has no size.

No Secrets

Do not keep secrets from each other. Instead, keep them for each other. Keep your private conversations between the two of you. Don't forget, she might only share certain information with certain people, so keep what she shared to yourself and let her decide who to share it with.

Speak in Person

It is essential to talk about subjects of great importance face to face. The true meaning of a message can get lost in a text, e-mail, and sometimes even over the phone. So make sure you are both heard and understood by talking face to face. To avoid misunderstandings, practice active listening. This is when you pay attention to what your partner is saying without interrupting or formulating your response. Then, repeat what your partner said back to them to ensure you understood them.

Earn Trust

Don't assume trust exists, and always work to earn it. When you stop taking trust for granted and make it a priority, you will be more conscious of your actions and how your behaviors affect your partner. When you commit to do something, make sure to do it. This way, your partner knows they can rely on you and trust you.

Practice Unconditional Acceptance and a Non-Judgmental Attitude

You might not understand why something is important to your partner, but the fact that it is important is all that matters. Before you can trust, you must respect each other and your differences without judgment. Just because you don't value certain things doesn't mean you should forget about them.

Be Vulnerable

Be honest with your partner. This sometimes means sharing things that you keep hidden. Trust is living your truth, and by doing so, your partner will be more comfortable living theirs.

Be Supportive

It is essential to be supportive of your partner. Supporting each other is most critical when trust is first forming. Supporting your partner when they are trying something new or acting outside their comfort zone can be very powerful. This shows your partner that they don't have to be just one way; you will love and support them even when they try new things and make mistakes trying them. Being supportive of your partner, whether in good times or bad, builds trust and allows you both to be who you are. Knowing your partner supports you regardless of your situation creates a strong bond.

Be Forgiving

Holding a resentment toward your partner is poisonous. Trusting doesn't mean mistakes won't happen - and when they do, be forgiving. Even those who love us can hurt us, either accidentally or intentionally. Sometimes when you or your partner are angry, you may say things you don't mean. Both of you need to be forgiving and loving regardless. Why? Because there must be faith in your bond. The only way to move forward is to forgive, especially those we love the most. You need to feel confident that you can make mistakes, be imperfect, and fall while enveloped in your partner's unconditional acceptance of who you are.

Be United

Disagreeing in public or in front of friends and family never goes over well. If you disagree with your partner, find time to talk later. Shaming your partner in front of others is mean, and as a loving, trustworthy partner, you must be vigilant in supporting your partner's self-worth. If you are parents, you need to be on the same page with your partner regarding child-rearing.

Practice Self-Care

You must practice self-care. Taking good care of yourself adds to the health of your relationship. You are a better person and better in your relationship when you take the time to care for and work on yourself. Sometimes this means you or your partner may need alone time to care for yourselves. It is essential to allow for this. You must grow both as an individual and as a couple.

Continuing to Grow

Growing your relationship takes time. Work daily to build trust. Be true to yourself by being truthful to your partner. Learn about your partner and what they expect of you. Only then can you decide if this is 'your person' - the person you want to stand with and support no matter what comes. I tell couples to stand together and face the world as one instead of turning on each other during stressful times. To build trust, you must be behaviorally consistent and do what you say you will do. Be forgiving and non-judgmental. Don't criticize your partner when they are not believing or acting as you do. Commit to accepting your partner fully. Love all of who they are – without condition, with your arms wide open and an accepting heart.

Reflections

_____

_____

_____

_____

_____

_____

_____

_____

_____

_____

_____

_____

_____

_____

_____

_____

_____

_____

_____

_____

_____

What changes do you want to make?

_____

_____

_____

_____

_____

_____

_____

What steps do you need to take to bring about change?

_____

_____

_____

_____

_____

_____

_____

_____

_____

_____

"If you promise to love, trust, respect, support, and stand by someone no matter what, do not just speak those words when times are good. Live those words when challenges arise. The stronger the love and commitment, the more unbreakable the bond. United hearts will never be easily divided."

— *Carlos Wallace*

24. LOVE AND COMMITMENT

Finding the Motivation To Change

Last week I had introductory counseling sessions with two different couples. In our meetings, I found that they behaved in similar ways. Couples don't often present for counseling so close to what I believe to be the end of the relationship. This seemed to be the case with both. Couples come to me with disagreements, integration failure, and dysfunctional ways of communicating. However, I always believe couples want to continue the relationship when they walk through my door. During my 30 years as a therapist, I have seen couples make dramatic changes to fix their relationship. I have seen people transform and find their way to greater happiness. Unfortunately, I doubted this was the case with either of these couples.

Couple One

The man was quiet, the woman was not. While completing my assessment, I felt the man did not understand why he was in my office. His fiancé, however, was angry throughout the session and was disrespectful toward him repeatedly. Her need, directly related to her screaming, was for him to change.

She wanted him to be more open, to bring romance back into the relationship, and to again "be with the man he once was." She wanted him to share more with her and not stay so quiet. Throughout our meeting, the man sat quietly, showing little emotion. I noticed him sinking deeper into my sofa as the session continued. After helping his fiancé calm her anger, I asked him to share. He said he was happy with the relationship as it is now. He accused her of living in the past. And, he griped, she wasn't the woman she once was as well. Ouch. He said he didn't understand what changes she wanted him to make, and the more she screamed, the more humiliated he became.

I steered the session in a workable direction, but they made little progress. Not much was accomplished during the session, and I suspected I would not see them again.

Couple Two

The second couple communicated more clearly than the first during their session, but not by much. They were newly married after a 10-year relationship. They argued throughout the session. The woman said he disrespects her with passive-aggressive behaviors. He would make snide comments about her family and complain every time they left the house.

He said he wasn't sure how he could continue in the relationship as she constantly blamed him for everything. He said she "always" picks her immediate family over him. She spends more time at her parent's house than home with him. He accused her of being just like her mother and pointed out that her parent's relationship had been over for years.

She fought back, saying that her family was wonderful and that she would be "thrilled" to have a marriage as good as her parents.

I scheduled return appointments for each couple for today, one right after the other.

To help a couple successfully repair and rebuild a relationship, I only need to know that each partner is committed to the other and that both are committed to making it work. Almost anything is possible if a couple is motivated to repair their relationship.

Couple One

I didn't expect couple one to show up for their appointment at all. But, surprisingly, they came. As we began, I immediately told them how to work active listening, that they needed to pay attention to each other and hear what they were saying to each other. They begrudgingly agreed to try. As each shared, I directed them as needed. Their communication showed improvement. When we were halfway through our session, I pointed out their behavior in our first meeting. I asked if they were committed to working on the relationship. They both told me they loved the other and were committed to the relationship. We spent the session negotiating changes each would make to improve the relationship.

195

Couple Two

The woman from couple two called me this morning and told me that she would not be coming to our session later today and was so mad at her spouse that she didn't see the point of coming. I encouraged her to come. To my surprise, they both came to the appointment.

Once the anger subsides, therapy can begin. Whether treatment is successful or not depends on motivation and willingness to change behaviors.

In the second session, couple two had the most difficulty. They ripped into each other, blamed each other, and threatened divorce (both of them at some point). She accused him of not being who she thought she married. He said the same thing back. However, by the end of the session, I was able to redirect them, and they did make some progress. They agreed to work on not picking at each other and not what I call "spit venom" at each other. "When you spit venom," I explained, "you are continually poisoning your relationship." They also agreed they would no longer threaten divorce unless they had a lawyer and were ready to file. It was no longer to be used as a weapon. They walked in hating each other and left with the motivation to change.

Commitment

To help a couple successfully repair and rebuild a relationship, I only need to know that each partner is committed to the other and that both are committed to making it work. Almost anything is possible if a couple is motivated to repair their relationship. Once the anger subsides, therapy can begin. Whether treatment is successful or not depends on motivation and willingness to change behaviors.

I always ask each partner to inventory their behaviors and identify what they are doing that is contributing to the relationship problems. I stress the need to work on a commitment to making changes based on the destructive behaviors they bring to the relationship. If they change their agreed-upon behaviors, there is much less to fight about. Once this takes place, fixing deeper relationship problems can begin.

Reflections

What changes do you want to make?

_____

_____

_____

_____

_____

_____

_____

What steps do you need to take to bring about change?

_____

_____

_____

_____

_____

_____

_____

_____

_____

"To be fully seen by somebody, then, and be loved anyhow - this is a human offering that can border on miraculous."

— *Elizabeth Gilbert*

25. YOUR RELATIONSHIP

What You Expect and What You Learn

"Why are you treating me this way?"

Sometimes your partner says things and acts in ways you don't understand. Things are supposed to be this way, not that way. Why doesn't he understand how things are supposed to be in a relationship? The answer is simple. Your understanding of how things should be in a relationship is different than your partner's. Your 'normal' is not their 'normal.'

You must accept that your partner's understanding of how relationships work – how to act, what to say, and how to handle things – will inevitably differ from yours. You have your own 'guide to relationships' in your head, while your partner has a different 'guide.' Their guide not only differs from yours but sometimes seems to be written in a different language. Why can't they see that your way is the right way and that their way is wrong?

Let Me Introduce You to Your Parents

Perhaps obvious but sometimes overlooked is the example your parents and caregivers set. During childhood, you learn how a relationship should be from the adults who raise you. If you thought everyone learned what a relationship is by watching "Leave It To Beaver" or "The Sopranos," you are mistaken.

To understand what your partner learned, examine their family and try to understand the 'rules' they have. Here you will find the underpinnings of your partners 'guide to relationships.' Then, look at your family – how you interact with each other, what you say to each other, how you behave – and recognize that much of what you believe to be a normal relationship was influenced by this example.

These are the cornerstones of your 'guide' to normal relationships. Even if you disagreed with or hated the nature of your caregiver's relationships, it was what you grew up with and was a primary example.

What Do We Do Now?

If the state of your relationship warrants, finding and working with an experienced and knowledgeable couples therapist is invaluable. Whether or not you work with a therapist, the first step is identifying your relationship goals. Work together to discover and outline the steps necessary to meet those goals. Issues such as conflicting relational definitions and beliefs must be identified and discussed.

Compromises will need to be made, and you may need to accept differing relational expectations. You may not agree with or even understand some of your partner's requests. The goal is to combine your two relationship guides into a new one – a relationship guide that you and your partner agree to. Commitment to change will be necessary, and a couples therapist can help you work on changing the behaviors you want to change.

When it comes to relationships, we learn the rules, the ways of interacting, and the ways of behaving - what a relationship is and how it works - from our parents and caregivers. Your 'normal' is what you learned, and your partner's 'normal' is what they learned.

For the relationship to thrive, you must learn to respect each other's boundaries, opinions, and individuality. These are essential for a healthy and intimate relationship to grow. It involves valuing your partner's feelings and treating them with kindness, empathy, and dignity.

Rewriting the foundation you and your partner have lived on is challenging and requires a commitment to the change process and each other. I have witnessed couples make incredible changes, turning dysfunctional relationships into happy, harmonious ones.

Every partnership is challenging. When difficulties arise, I strongly encourage you to examine your core beliefs about relationships. What were you taught, and what do you believe? Identify where you learned how relationships should be and how it affects your partnership today. Relationships should be joyful, strong partnerships. Work together, never apart, to create a more intimate bond.

Reflections

_____

_____

_____

_____

_____

_____

_____

_____

_____

_____

_____

_____

_____

_____

_____

_____

_____

_____

What changes do you want to make?

_____

_____

_____

_____

_____

_____

_____

What steps do you need to take to bring about change?

_____

_____

_____

_____

_____

_____

_____

_____

_____

_____

"You know you're in love when you can't fall asleep because reality is finally better than your dreams."

— *Dr. Seuss*

26. CHOOSING A PARTNER

Finding Your Person

Choosing to be together forever is one of life's greatest joys. It is life-changing and one of the most critical choices you will make. Yet, it is essential to recognize that this choice - a choice that will change your life forever – is often powerfully influenced by feelings of true love and the rapture of sex. But, choosing to commit to your partner may seem so obvious that, at the time, you don't realize that you are choosing at all. You are in love, and you can't imagine being apart.

Forever

When you and your partner formally commit to each other, you make promises that remind you that you aren't being forced to be together. You are choosing to be together, and some responsibilities come along with that choice. You promise to love and support each other no matter what. You have chosen to live with this person forever, to stand by them and care for them no matter what life may bring. By doing this, you have also made another choice you may not have recognized at all. By committing to your partner, you are choosing to accept them completely and without condition - forever.

If you commit to your partner and accept them for who they are — not who you wish they would be or become - happiness and joy can be found.

This means that annoying habits and selfish acts by your partner don't excuse you from accepting them for who they are. You may snore; she may hide chocolate. I have been married for a while now, and when I look back at our beginnings, I didn't fully understand that choosing to commit demands choosing to accept. It does, and it is essential.

Optimism

This is an example of how you sometimes make choices without knowing all there is to know. As a human, you tend to be optimistic — you believe that tomorrow will be better than yesterday. Therefore, certain choices you make may look unshakable when you make them. However, you cannot predict what will happen as you don't know what the future may bring.

Of course, you do your best to make informed choices. But history repeatedly shows that there is no such thing as a sure thing. However, happiness and joy can be found if you commit to your partner and accept them for who they are — not who you wish they would be or become. The waters do not drown you even when bad choices lead to horrific life problems. A relational foundation built on mutual commitment and acceptance will provide the buoyancy needed to stay afloat.

When Difficulties Arise

Each day I work with people struggling with life challenges. My clients and I work on sad, painful, and extremely difficult problems. My life has taught me that a few unimaginable challenges may lie ahead. During these difficult times, you and your partner must stay close, accept difficult situations as they come, and treat each other with kindness and respect.

Use the strength inherent in your relationship to face the world together and not turn on each other. Great power is inherent in your commitment to love and accept one another. I often meet with couples who have turned against each other. The relationship is slowly poisoned by mean words and deeds when this happens. When couples turn against each other, their commitment can collapse, and as each blames the other, all feelings of love vanish.

Be careful with blame when challenges arise. One of you may have made a wrong or hurtful choice, but if you choose to stay together, you must face your difficulties and support each other.

It's normal to wonder if you chose to marry who you married at all. "Did I spend enough time thinking about whether I could spend the rest of my life with this person?" This question can never be answered with any certainty. Regardless of who you may think you should have married instead, remember that this person is also imperfect. Never forget that we're all human, and all humans, by design, are imperfect.

This is Us

When my wife and I chose to get married, I thought I had great wisdom, having worked with so many couples over my career. I felt that our marriage would be continual bliss. I knew what I was doing. HA! I was wrong, of course. My marriage does reveal an essential truth to me, one that defines what choice and commitment are all about: to find happiness, you must accept your partner for who they are.

Acceptance

Our first date was having brunch at Philadelphia's excellent Sabrina's Café. It was a Sunday morning, and the line to get into the place, like every Sunday, ran down the block. I waited patiently for her. While in line, my phone rang - 15 minutes past our agreed-upon meeting time - it was her. "Sorry, I'm running late. I'm driving over the bridge now."

Okay, 15 minutes is within normal parameters. Another 15 minutes pass. I'm still waiting, inching close to the front of the line. Another call: "I'm almost there. See you soon." Minutes pass, and I'm now at the front of the line. But my date had still not arrived.

I explained this to the hostess, who was kind enough to sit me alone at a table in the middle of the restaurant. I ordered some fruit. And I waited. I see people in line giving me the evil eye, wondering why I'm dawdling with a bowl of fruit when they're waiting to eat some of Sabrina's delicious stuffed French toast.

She finally arrives! We smile at each other as she sits down. "Sorry I'm late! Oooooooo! Fruit!" Suddenly a forked hand reaches across the table, snatching fruit from my bowl. At that moment, I felt like I had known her my entire life. I never believed in 'love at first sight,' but I knew she was the one.

After a few dates, we met at her house. I discovered a house cluttered with piles of this and that and a few dust balls dancing in the corners. But soon, I fell deeply in love. Her cluttered house and dust balls did not matter. This was the most wonderful person I had ever met.

Meant To Be

It didn't take long for her to realize what I had on the day we had first met: that our being together was "bashert" - Yiddish for "meant to be."

Eventually, I stumbled upon a great truth: if I marry this person, I must accept everything about her. I realized that if I decided to marry her, I would not have the right to yell if we were running late for, well, everything. I would have to accept her organizationally-challenged nature, and I would have to live my life in a disorganized house. To marry this person - and find happiness - I would need to accept all of who she was and never expect her to be who she was not - ever. And I would have to live with my choice forever. I suspect she had this same realization.

The day before our wedding, I came home and, stumbling in the dark, discovered that our electricity had been shut off. Even though we had enough to pay the electric bill, the bride forgot to pay it. So, I fumbled around and asked, "Okay, what do we have to do to get the electricity back on?" She replied, "This is why I'm marrying you. You love me just the way I am." She will deny ever saying this, but she did.

Our Choices

We make many choices each day. If they are good ones, be grateful. If they are wrong, expect a mess, but remember that we all make mistakes. However, we alone make our choices, and we must own our choices. Choice equals freedom. When we accept responsibility for our choices and do our best to choose wisely, we can live the life we imagine. When it comes to your relationship, be careful not to make the biggest mistake I hear in my office every day: expecting your partner to be who they are not and blaming them for *your choice*.

Reflections

_____

_____

_____

_____

_____

_____

_____

_____

_____

_____

_____

_____

_____

_____

_____

_____

_____

_____

_____

What changes do you want to make?

_____

_____

_____

_____

_____

_____

_____

What steps do you need to take to bring about change?

_____

_____

_____

_____

_____

_____

_____

_____

_____

_____

"I want to be in a relationship where you telling me you love me is just a ceremonious validation of what you already show me."

— *Steve Maraboli*

27. BEST FRIENDS

The Most Important Part of Couplehood

We know that marriage and committed relationships have their problems. When it comes to relationships, good communication has been seen as the most critical issue. However, many therapists believe that friendship is the most essential part of a happy and satisfying relationship. I agree.

Good friends are those who love and support you when you need them. And you are there to love and support them when they need you. These are what I call your "inner circle" people. Your inner circle sometimes includes family members and always includes friends.

Your inner circle, however, only contains trustworthy people. It does not include people who gossip about you or don't return your texts. Your inner circle people are those you can call whenever you have an emergency, and they will be there. Your inner circle supports you when you are overwhelmed by life circumstances or internal struggles. Those who gossip about you or hurt you in other ways aren't friends. They may be fun to be around, so you may not cut your connection to them altogether. But they are unreliable, and you know they won't be there for you when you need them.

If you are married or in a relationship and aren't with someone you would consider an inner circle friend, it is time to begin marriage or relationship counseling.

If you are not married to or in a relationship with an inner circle friend, it is time to begin marriage or relationship counseling. A primary focus of counseling should be to rekindle the friendship that was so important at the beginning of your relationship.

Your Needs: What Does It Mean To Be Best Friends Again?

Trust

In some relationships, the friendship ended years ago. The first area to focus on is trusting your partner. You need to work on feeling comfortable sharing your thoughts and emotions. If you can't trust your partner, you can't comfortably share your thoughts and feelings. You will be unable to turn to your partner when you need support.

Communicate

Do you communicate successfully? Friends can communicate clearly. Watch out for mind-reading. This is when you expect your partner to know what you need and want without you asking for it. Yelling at each other is an obvious example of poor communication. When you shout, you push your partner away. The only thing you are communicating is your anger. Improving your relationship requires communicating so that you hear and understand each other.

Spend Time Together

How well do you know your partner? If you have been living separate lives, you must begin to spend more time together and be willing to do things your partner wants to do even when you don't want to do them.

Support Each Other

When examining your marriage or relationship, look for passive-aggressive behaviors such as demeaning comments or anger that seems to come out sideways (judgmental comments here and there). Do you share your successes with your partner? Or are you afraid of being mocked or belittled when celebrating the positive side of yourself? If you are experiencing these problems, participating in marital or relationship counseling can help. Being mean to each other doesn't nurture your friendship and, in severe cases, can lead to contempt - a hole most couples find impossible to escape.

But, when you find your way back to friendship, you become committed to supporting each other when you are struggling or need someone to be there. Instead of making a snide comment when your partner reaches out, you provide what you would expect from a friend. You provide love and care for each other in times of need. You share the good things as well as the bad. Being there for each other creates a sense of safety and security. Knowing that you are not alone and are connected intimately with another person is a powerful feeling. Friendship lets you live more comfortably because you know you have a supportive, loving partner who will be there to support you.

Do Things You Both Like

What do you have in common? What things did you like doing earlier in the relationship? Start doing those things that you have in common. Have a date night. Surprise your partner with tickets to a concert. Go on a trip to a place you've both dreamed of going. Being friends means finding and enjoying shared interests and making the time to do them. Rediscover having fun together.

Be Romantic

When was the last time you had sex? That's only part of creating greater intimacy and emotional connection, but it can be significant. To become physically intimate again, start acting as you did at the beginning of your relationship. When you trust your partner, being physically intimate becomes easier, especially if you haven't been sexual in a while. Trust also allows both of you to share your secret desires - which can lead to new and exciting ways to connect. Uncovering past emotional connections makes getting physically close safer and easier.

Be Committed

Sometimes when I work with couples, I can feel fear in the room. One or both of you may fear your partner will end the relationship. The road to greater security is rekindling your friendship. You demonstrate your commitment to the relationship when you understand each other again and renew your friendship. When you begin to like and respect each other again, you create deeper emotional intimacy and commitment. As friends, you will be committed to facing difficult times together, not blaming each other for the problem.

Watch Out For Unmet Expectations

Unhappiness lives in unmet expectations. Most relationships struggle with this. We have expectations and are unhappy when our partner fails to meet them. Is your partner really inconsiderate, or do you sometimes mind-read, expecting your partner to know what you want and expect from them without asking? Fixing this can be as simple as asking for what you need and want instead of expecting your partner to know what you need and want. If you struggle with asking for what you need, this will take practice. But, if you don't speak up, sometimes your expectations will not be met. In counseling, you can discuss each other's needs and agree to make changes to support each other.

Your daily commitment to your partner is the most critical decision you make each day. If you struggle with this commitment, take an inventory of why. Then, address your relationship struggles and work to become best friends again.

Reflections

_____

_____

_____

_____

_____

_____

_____

_____

_____

_____

_____

_____

_____

_____

_____

_____

_____

_____

_____

_____

_____

What changes do you want to make?

_____

_____

_____

_____

_____

_____

_____

_____

What steps do you need to take to bring about change?

_____

_____

_____

_____

_____

_____

_____

_____

_____

_____

"First I see and think I love, then I say I know I love, today and forever more I decide to love."

— Michael Sweeney

28. SECRET LOVE

Creating a Love That Lasts

It will happen. You will meet your perfect partner. Attentive, caring, loving, sexy – your soul mate. You access your list of 'must haves' on your smartphone. We've all made one, or perhaps given up on one – but the list is the list! Your perfect partner must have certain qualities, and, as a pragmatic romantic, compromise doesn't seem logical. That ideal person is out there, and you have faith that they will arrive and make your dreams a reality. So, where is the secret love you dream about?

They stand before you – perfection! Playful courting ensues, and your brain transforms. The love chemicals take hold, and full-blown infatuation overtakes every cell of your body. You both fall hard and soon find that everything has changed. You are ecstatic, and the high of infatuating love is convincing. This is your person.

It's happening, and you find the relationship so intoxicating, intense, and intimate that you are convinced that being rational is ridiculous. The belief that love conquers all leads the way. And the sex – most, if not all of us, have experienced the rapture - the sexual pleasure accompanying the early months of newfound love is wonderful.

You flirt, play, laugh, show affection, and support each other fully. You accept one another unconditionally, forgive imperfections, and tend to work out problems in a giving and selfless way.

Transitioning

New love can turn your hopes and dreams into a reality you see as clear as day. It brings out the best in you. But remember, infatuation makes it easy to bury and hide the person you really are. It's also easy for your new partner to show their best side in this early stage. Infatuation clouds your vision.

Soon, the intensity of your newfound love lessens, and you start to notice that your new partner isn't so perfect. And you begin to reveal your imperfections. A few months into new relationships, neurotransmitter levels in our brains normalize. After a few years, most of the chemical bomb that exploded early on is gone. What's next? How do you create lasting love?

Lasting Love

Be sure you remember all the wonderful things that occur during the infatuation stage of your relationship. The underpinnings of true and lasting love can be found by examining your beginnings. For example, during infatuation, we almost always put our new love's needs before anything else, and we find it easy to lovingly forgive our partner when something goes wrong.

Love is more often a verb than a noun. Love is action, and love grows through loving action. It's not enough to say, 'I love you.' You need to act in ways that demonstrate your love – be considerate, caring, and respectful of your partner. Infatuation fades but continued loving actions lead to the growth of mature love.

To create lasting love, you must be vigilant. Look for signs that your relationship may need attention or is taking unhealthy turns. These include being less willing to make time to be together or when you no longer give your partner the benefit of the doubt. You begin jumping to conclusions and blaming them. Perhaps you start feeling that you are 'falling out of love.'

If your expectations are that the intensity of infatuated love will last forever, then you are certain to be disappointed. As a result, you may miss the opportunity to create a mature, loving relationship. The key to happiness is aligning your expectations with reality and committing to the hard work that love requires.

Expectations

After the infatuation stage passes, you will see your relationships more clearly. You must now accept that the intensity of emotions experienced during infatuation fades and that infatuation is not true love.

Happiness lives in what you have together, not in what you wish you had. If your expectations are that the intensity of infatuated love will last forever, then you are certain to be disappointed. You may miss the opportunity to create a mature, loving relationship. The key to happiness is aligning your expectations with reality and committing to the hard work that love requires.

As Love Grows

As your relationship matures, you will recognize that you share some of the same values and goals. Living together forever does require planning for the future. Do you want a family? How much money do you and your partner desire? Where do you want to live? Innumerable questions get answered along the way. But, the path you and your partner decide to follow needs to be a shared vision. In mature relationships, partners negotiate and agree on their goals and work together to complete the steps they must take to achieve them.

Commit to loving - and acting in loving ways - each day. As our needs as humans change with time, love must also change.

Over time, relationships need to be able to change and adjust. Life does not follow a straight path, and a mature couple recognizes and prepares for this. You must be flexible when it comes to roles and responsibilities. Your role today may not be the one you must fulfill tomorrow.

Compromising is crucial. You are still two people, and you will not agree on everything. Be prepared to follow life's path, as this may not be the path you envisioned early on.

Commit to loving - and acting in loving ways - each day. As our needs as humans change with time, love must also change. Continuing to act in loving ways as your love matures is the key to creating love that grows.

Love begins as an explosion of human chemistry. But, when attended to properly, love matures, grows, and becomes far more significant than a feeling. True love is action. It is how you respect and attend to your partner. Love is a life lived together - and ultimately - as one.

Reflections

_____

_____

_____

_____

_____

_____

_____

_____

_____

_____

_____

_____

_____

_____

_____

_____

_____

_____

_____

_____

_____

What changes do you want to make?

_____

_____

_____

_____

_____

_____

_____

_____

What steps do you need to take to bring about change?

_____

_____

_____

_____

_____

_____

_____

_____

_____

_____

Made in the USA
Middletown, DE
05 July 2023

34507496R00139